# A THOUSAND VOICES

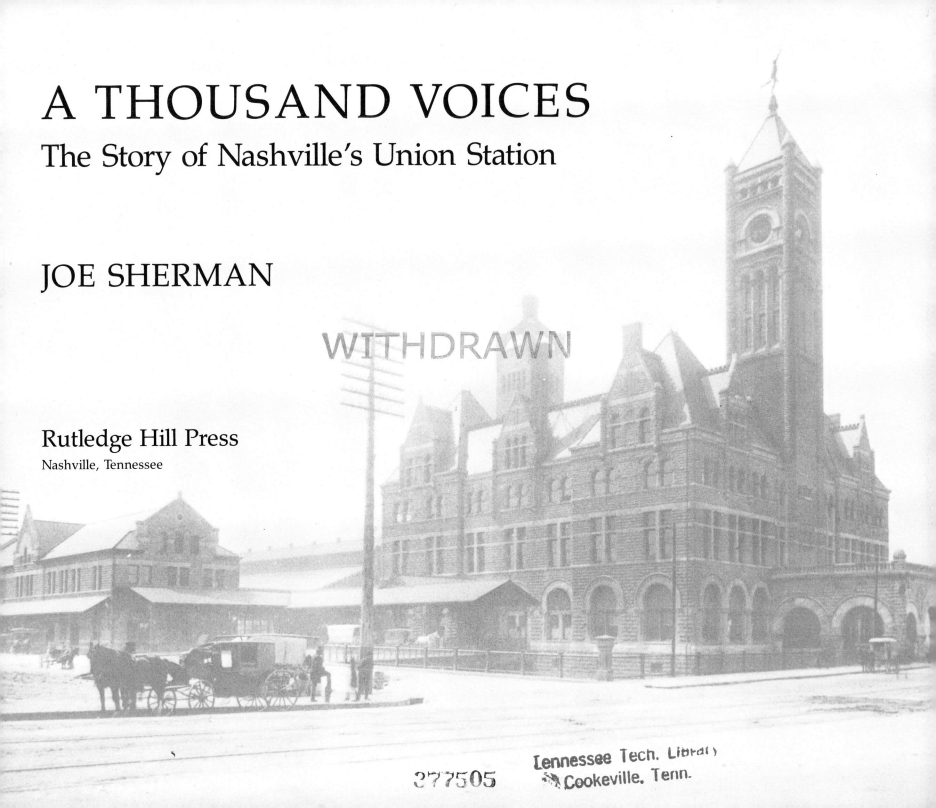

# A THOUSAND VOICES
The Story of Nashville's Union Station

JOE SHERMAN

WITHDRAWN

**Rutledge Hill Press**
Nashville, Tennessee

Published in Nashville, Tennessee, by Rutledge Hill Press, Inc., 513 Third Avenue South, Nashville, Tennessee 37210

Typography by ProtoType Graphics, Inc.
Designed by Harriette Bateman
Printed by Parthenon Press

**Library of Congress Cataloging-in-Publication Data**

Sherman, Joe, 1945–
  A thousand voices.

  Bibliography: p.
  Includes index.
  1. Union Station (Nashville, Tenn.)   I. Title.
II. Title: 1000 voices.
TF302.N17S54   1987      385′.314′0976855      87–9700
ISBN 0-934395-49-7

Manufactured in the United States of America
1   2   3   4   5   6   7   8   9   10   —   92   91   90   89   88   87

# Contents

1.  An Opening Conflict      9

2.  Architectural Design      17

3.  Building a Landmark      21

4.  Alligator Pools, A Digital Clock, and Mercury      33

5.  The City and Its Station      41

6.  The Only Way to Travel      49

7.  Working There      59

8.  Hard Times, Great Visitors      71

9.  World War II      77

10. From Pullmans to Pontiacs      85

11. Pigeons and Politicians      91

12. A Ruin Transformed      99

*Floor Plans*      113

*Acknowledgements*      117

*Illustrations*      119

*References*      121

*Index*      123

# Dedication

This book is for Bea and Percy Cohen

# A THOUSAND VOICES

9, 13
17, 19, 21, 27
27, 23, 25, 40, 52
30, 32, 35, 69, 90
71, 75, 95, 96
91, 93, 97, 99, 108, 110, 111

# An Opening Conflict

Early in the morning of October 9, 1900, watering wagons appeared on Broad Street and began wetting down the dust. A huge parade was to begin at 9:00 and Union Station would formally open an hour later with music, ceremonies and speeches. At noon the street fair would start. There would be fireworks at 12:30 and a concert at 2:00. The fireworks would be repeated that evening, followed by another concert. To amuse the crowds the New England Carnival was in Nashville with rides, trained animals, Bosco the snake eater, Lunette the flying lady, and an Indian fortune teller. The American Vaudeville Theatre with its special attraction, the renowned Tyrolean warblers, was also in town for the great occasion.

Decades of delays were over. An impressive railroad station with a statue on the roof, a digital clock in the tower, and bare-breasted angels inside proclaimed that Nashville was joining the twentieth century.

As captains and crew members watched from the decks of their steamboats, parade marshals organized bands, wagons, animals and people on Front Street, which paralleled the Cumberland River. Drivers made last min-

ute adjustments to flowers on the spokes of carriage wheels. Impatient horses shook their traces, scattering petals from their manes.

The parade began on time. Steamboat whistles blew.

Major Eugene Castner Lewis, the man most responsible for Union Station, rode in a victoria, a low rig with a liveried driver seated high in front. Major Lewis was the hero of the hour. His skills and tenacity were the reason Union Station was opening on time. His nemesis, Colonel Jere Baxter, rode a black charger farther back in the parade, behind dignitaries, railroad officials, and politicians in forty-five carriages. Colonel Baxter accompanied the young ladies from Ward's Seminary, twenty of them, all dressed in white and crowded aboard a large tally-ho carriage. Dozens of society ladies in long-sleeved gowns and elaborate hats, some resting parasols on their shoulders to protect their stylish pallor from the sun, followed in landaus, broughams and Brewster rigs. Next came bands, mounted members of the Nashville police and fire departments on their best brushed steeds, and uniformed veterans of the Confederacy, a few supporting themselves with canes. Six hun-

*Major Eugene Castner Lewis*

dred banner-waving workers from the railroad shops and yards followed in order, some of them already smelling of the alcohol they had been sharing in celebration of their new jobs.

Flags and bunting decorated the parade route. Both sides of Broad Street teemed with spectators. Children balanced on their fathers' shoulders and peeped between the legs of adults.

At the station fifteen hundred chairs were lined up beneath the shed. Hundreds of people stood around the sides. The veterans found their reserved seats in the front. To the accompaniment of music from the Marine Band, the dignitaries ascended the central staircase to the grand concourse with the girls from Ward's behind them.

As was his habit when introduced at public gatherings, August Belmont from New York merely rose and bowed. As chairman of the board of the Louisville and Nashville Railroad, he was the man responsible for the money that built the station; its completion spoke eloquently enough for him. He was followed by Milton Smith, president of the L&N, and by Major John W. Thomas, president of the Nashville, Chattanooga and St. Louis Railroad, or the NC&St L as the subsidiary of the L&N was called.

To loud applause Major Lewis took the rostrum. Not comfortable in front of this many people, he simply told the crowd that the station spoke in a thousand voices, all they had to do was listen, and left it at that.

Then the mayor of Nashville, James H. Head, stood to speak, and a little tension

brittled the air. For years Mayor Head had aligned himself with Colonel Jere Baxter and his Tennessee Central Railroad against Major Lewis and the L&N. Both Head and Baxter thought Nashville should have its own railroad, one owned and managed by Tennesseans, rather than the L&N, which was owned by New Yorkers like Belmont and operated out of Louisville. In fact, the previous week, the two had won the endorsement of the Nashville city council to put a bond issue before the voters which, if passed, would give a million dollars to the Tennessee Central. Prompting the endorsement was the fact that the L&N had refused the upstart Tennessee Central access to the new Union Station.

In his remarks Mayor Head praised the station, saying it meant great things for the future. He invited businessmen to locate in Nashville, a city of abundant resources. Then he admitted having been a little doubtful that Union Station would ever be finished. However, now that it was, he urged August Belmont and the other railroad magnates to look upon Nashville "not as a lemon to be squeezed, nor even as a rich harvest to be gathered, but as a fertile field to be cared for and cultivated." Gesturing toward the statue of Mercury high above their heads, he concluded by saying, "May the winged messenger of the immortals, whose figure adorns the top of this building, in his eagerness to promote [Nashville commerce] forget the fighting, theft and thievery going on all around."

There were some coughs, a few rubbed necks, some shifting in chairs. Major Lewis

*Railroad officials, politicians, school girls, society ladies, firemen and policemen, bands, Confederate veterans, and banner-waving railroad workers participated in the opening day parade.*

11

*The old depot at Church and Walnut streets (now Tenth Avenue).*

glanced at Mayor Head as though he could have sprung on him.

In the audience Colonel Baxter smiled to himself. Let Major Lewis, Belmont and the others squirm a little. They deserved it.

Just recently, when the Tennessee Central had tried to gain access to the new station, a flurry of free train rides and gifts (favored lobbying methods of the era) had suddenly come the way of politicians and lawyers whose support the L&N needed to bar the tracks to competition. The lobbying effort had both worked, because the Tennessee Central was shut out, and backfired, because it re-

minded Nashville of what the L&N would do to keep a hometown railroad from getting established. Sympathy for the underdog, which had waned the past few years while the L&N had helped finance the state's Centennial Exposition of 1897 and built Union Station, had suddenly swung Colonel Baxter's way. Voters would soon approve the million dollar bond issue for the Tennessee Central. Then subsequent lawsuits would mire Baxter's railroad down and waste away its resources.

On this day, though, the future of the local line looked bright. It appeared that Colonel Baxter, the so-called "Napoleon of the South," had the giant L&N on the run.

Mayor Head took his seat and a large urn was placed in front of the seated dignitaries. Prim and proper in their white dresses, the young ladies from Ward's Seminary rose to represent the angels of Tennessee commerce. As each brought a product forward, such as flour, corn, lumber, whiskey and iron, to place in the urn, they were dramatizing the symbolism of the angels looking down from the walls of the main waiting room. Much later in life two of these girls, Saidee Cauvin and Frances McLester, recalled the ceremony.

"It was an *event*," Cauvin said. "I knew they were going to take all the older girls, and I didn't expect to be taken, and finally when I found out I was going, I was very pleased. And the thing that amazes me is that I can *still* remember. . . . Anyway, I believe they had a parade...[and] we were in a tally-ho. . . . I know we had to wear white dresses."

"We went down as a group," McLester said, "and sat on the platform there at the junction of the two [staircases]. . . . And we in turn got up to speak about the various agricultural products of Tennessee. I know one of my friends had a little reel of cotton. . . . She rose and showed the bale of cotton and held it high. I think I got the hops from my own trees on my front yard."

"My, some of them had a lot to say," Cauvin remembered about the verses they recited, "but I didn't. I had a piece of iron ore, and I was to say, 'Iron, the best of metals and the pride of minerals.' And that was my entire business!"

The noon concert followed. Dignitaries boarded their carriages and rode to the Maxwell House hotel for a banquet. There, stirred up by Mayor Head's remarks, August Belmont addressed the businessmen of Nashville.

The public toured the station, peered up at Mercury and the digital clock, and descended to the shed to imagine journeys aboard the private Pullmans in which Belmont, Smith and others had arrived. Later, they could ride the world's smallest working locomotive on the midway of the New England Carnival. It pulled a miniature train around seven hundred feet of track while the Ferris wheel whirled overhead and mothers propped their children on the wooden horses of the merry-go-round. Barkers extolled the wonders of the flying lady and the snake eater and encouraged everyone to come to the tents and buy tickets.

*Major Lewis's home on Belmont Boulevard.*

Everyone was in a good mood. Finally, Nashville had a modern railroad station. It stood two hundred and thirty-seven feet, including Mercury, and was one hundred and fifty feet square. It cost $300 thousand. The shed cost an additional $200 thousand. Several hundred employees would soon start working in the building. Many times that number were newly hired in the surrounding yards. Union Station centered a web of steel that spread to all the cities in Tennessee and via connecting lines to every state in the Union. The L&N, despite its past, had put on a good show. Looking back at the decades of conflict between Nashville and the L&N, it was easy to understand the sense of elation.

*Three hundred and fifty feet long and one hundred feet wide, the Machinery Building drew tens of thousands inside to see engines, boilers and generators.*

The original hard feelings between the two had started in the late 1870s when the father of the railroad in Tennessee, Vernon K. Stevenson, had sold control of the NC&St L to the L&N. For years the L&N maintained the scattered passenger and freight facilities that had been built in Nashville before and after the War Between the States, but made no move to build a new station. Although the old depot had impressed visitors to frontier Nashville in 1850, it was outdated, crowded, and ready for replacement by 1880. By then Nashville was regaining its economic vitality after the difficult years of Reconstruction and up-to-date railroad facilities were necessary to sustain growth.

To understand the importance of a new station, one must remember that in the late nineteenth century, railroads practically defined commerce. To bestow prosperity on a city, the railroad passed through it; to guarantee decline, the railroad passed by or allowed facilities to become outdated. Most things that moved any distance—raw materials, manufactured goods, services or people—went by rail. As an imposing oak is defined by its branches, the outline of a region's commerce was defined by its railroad lines. The farther a city was from trunk lines, the more marginal its commerce and the more dubious its future.

Businessmen in Nashville no longer wanted to be dubious of the city's future. They wanted good transportation because good transportation meant trade. And trade meant progress. If they were to compete with their counterparts in Louisville, Atlanta, Birmingham and other cities of the central South, the rail facilities had to expand. The key to that expansion was a new station.

The L&N postponed building one throughout the 1880s, however. Its management spent large sums of money fighting federal regulation of its growth, while Nashville made do with facilities that were becoming more and more outdated.

Then in 1892 Major Eugene Castner Lewis appeared and made it known that the L&N was changing its attitude. He started spending money, acquiring property, and showing himself to be a man who got things done.

At first Major Lewis kept his wife Pauline and their seven children in Sycamore, Tennessee, where he remained president of a powder plant that made explosives, and traveled back and forth to Nashville on railroad business. While in the city he also began construction of an unusual house. From the outside it suggested Frank Lloyd Wright's Prairie Style, which the architect was just developing. On the inside the house was all curved surfaces finished in fine oak, cherry and other hardwoods; it was said that the major preferred curved surfaces so that his children would never bang their heads against sharp edges.

During his first years in Nashville, Major Lewis was criticized by Colonel Jere Baxter and supporters of the Tennessee Central. They challenged his intentions, derided the fact he worked for the L&N, and mocked his statements. Early in 1896, once Major Lewis announced his intention to build Union Station, a reporter for the *Nashville Daily Sun*, a paper that supported the Tennessee Central, wrote: "The union depot will require 200 men two years to complete it, according to Mr. Lewis. That is too dazzling for our untrained imagination. The suggestion that it will take 200 years to get two men started to work on the union depot would strike us as more probable. . . . Wait until after the Centennial, says Mr. Lewis. Until after which Centennial, that of [1897] or that of [1997]?"

Baxter and his supporters may have been worried about the future of their fledgling Tennessee Central. The worse the L&N's reputation in Nashville, the better for them. Now the L&N was both pouring money into the upcoming Centennial Exposition, an event it

*A wood, plaster and stucco replica of the Parthenon became the centerpiece of the Centennial Exposition of 1897.*

had seized upon as an opportunity to reverse its poor reputation in Nashville, and saying it would start Union Station afterwards. In fact, Major Lewis had already been named director-general of the exposition and was in the process of taking firm command.

Convinced the exposition lacked a symbolic and unifying theme, Major Lewis proposed an idea for one at a Centennial committee meeting. He said, "About the center, on an elevation that will have to be supplied, I want to put a reproduction of the Parthenon,

15

in actual size, line for line, and call it the Fine Arts Building."

The conservative committee members glanced around at each other, a bit dazed by Major Lewis's audacity.

"I'll be damned," one declared.

Another, recently returned from Greece, said, "I don't know why you want to reproduce that thing—it's nothing but a tumble-down piece of rubbish."

Nevertheless, a replica of the Parthenon was soon under construction. Major Lewis had located and bought two large volumes of plans for the monument from the British Museum for five hundred dollars. He had also obtained rights to recreate the design from the King of Greece.

The Centennial opened on May 1, 1897, when, in a bit of wizardry for the time, President William McKinley put his finger to a button in Washington, D.C., and a cannon went off in West Side Park (now called Centennial Park) in Nashville.

The exposition offered something for everyone. An impressive array of temporary buildings complemented the classical lines of the Parthenon. Plying manmade Lake Watauga were hatted gondoliers in their gondolas, both imported from Venice by Major Lewis. For the adventurous there was a giant slide down which they plunged into a shallow pool and a giant seesaw that lifted them two hundred feet into the air. There were camels from Egypt to ride and belly dancers from the Near East to admire. The Parthenon and a replica of the Great Pyramid of Giza, both built of stucco, plaster and wood, towered into the air, with strands of lights silhouetting them at night. There were exhibition buildings and a midway. President and Mrs. McKinley came by train and toured the grounds. Over a period of five months, hundreds of thousands of people came to Nashville by rail, buggy, bicycle, horseback or on foot to see and be seen, to marvel at the sights from their century and the next, and to be entertained by the drama and the excitement.

The Centennial Exposition was the biggest spectacle Tennessee had ever seen, and after it closed Major Lewis's reputation rose like a helium balloon. The small and dapper man who preferred not to talk much had helped revitalize the economy of Nashville, had whitewashed the reputation of the L&N, had created a public park that would become the nucleus of Nashville's visionary public park system, and had given the city the perfect symbol for its reputation as the "Athens of the South." Triumphant and confident, he now wielded tremendous power to influence the future.

Riding this momentum he pushed the Depot Bill through the Nashville city council in June, 1898, and the stage was set for the construction of Union Station.

# Architectural Design

Why the L&N chose one of Henry Hobson Richardson's buildings, the Allegheny County Courthouse in Pittsburgh, as the model for Union Station is a good question. It probably came down to the fact that in the late 1890s Richardson was in vogue; his buildings also had authority, historical roots, and were labeled uniquely American—three elements close to a railroad baron's heart.

Richardson was a southerner by birth (he was born in Louisiana in 1838), had a speech impediment, and spent four years at Harvard College. Although his grades were mediocre, he cultivated friendships there that served him well the rest of his life. His first jobs were designing lamps and supervising construction projects. He won a commission in 1866, setting him on a course that would over a period of twenty years make him the most respected architect in America, and possibly the world. When Richardson died at age forty-seven of Bright's disease, a kidney ailment, he left behind many imitators. His masterpieces included the William Watts Sherman house in Newport, Rhode Island, Trinity Church in Boston's Back Bay, the New York state capitol, the Marshall Field's wholesale store (now demolished) in Chicago, and the Allegheny County Buildings.

To achieve his singular style Richardson did not look to the future for his ideas, but rather to the distant past. Most architects of his time were doing the same, robbing the medieval manor house of the Middle Ages in England for layout and form. They liked this precedent because the previous century had saddled them with stiff classical styles and the manor house was relatively informal; it gave them a much needed freedom.

Richardson did them one step further. He focused on an earlier style, the Romanesque.

Romanesque had flourished in Western Europe from about 800 to 1200. Early in its development it usually appeared in low, severe churches with thick walls, heavy columns, and arched windows and doors. Builders worked from the remains of the Roman Empire scattered throughout the countryside. They stalked through arches and along crumbling arcades, and scrutinized ruins from centuries before. These builders worked on the trial-and-error method and endured many collapsed walls before discovering technical breakthroughs. Their eventual

use of the flying buttress evolved Romanesque into the light, airy Gothic style where ribbed vaults were supported by slender pillars, large expanses of stained glass told biblical tales, and flying buttresses held the structure aloft, often at a great height.

As an outgrowth of Romanesque, Gothic took centuries to achieve unique form and to become divorced from its predecessor. Accordingly, Romanesque came to mean an architectural style lacking a certain perfection, a style on its way to a higher level of achievement.

That Romanesque lacked the perfection of Gothic, which was widely imitated in neo-Gothic during the nineteenth century, did not seem to bother H.H. Richardson. He embraced the outstanding characteristics of the older style: strength and heaviness through the use of rounded (Roman) arches, massive piers and walls, and the barrel and groin vaults for interior supports. In the process he achieved a dignity and simplicity in his buildings and created a style all his own.

His larger works were rugged and magnificent masonry boxes that emphasized the wholeness of the building rather than its features. He loved stone and avoided ornamentation. A typical Richardson building was massive and powerful, yet subdued; it radiated a sense of imposing calm.

By the late 1890s, though, more than a decade after the architect's death, the use of his Allegheny County Courthouse in Pittsburgh as a model was far from daring. America's first skyscrapers were appearing in

Opposite page: *The Allegheny County Courthouse in Pittsburgh served as the model for Union Station.*

*This original blueprint shows details of the porte-cochère beneath which travelers drove their carriages and redcaps unloaded their trunks.*

Chicago at this time and architecture was beginning a period of upheaval. Yet August Belmont and most railroad barons preferred structures less adventurous than the sky-scrapers that elevators, steel framing, and a leap of the imagination made possible. The look of authority and power they preferred in railroad stations got along fine with more historic designs and materials. Concerns of the newer architects for such things as improved lighting, ventilation and interior function were also deemed less important than ruggedness, mass and size. Recent advances in construction, like central heating, hot and cold water, sanitary plumbing, and gas and electric lights, could be fit as easily in historical frameworks as into modern ones.

Richard Montfort, chief engineer for the L&N, received credit for the design of Union Station, while Major Lewis added his personal touches: the artistic interior, the alligator pools, the digital clock, and Mercury. One question about the design, however, concerns the role that Montfort actually played in it.

That the L&N placed Montfort, who was a civil engineer by training, in charge of design was not out of the ordinary, nor was his method of borrowing from a recently dead master that odd in this era of historical plundering. What is puzzling is the fact that Montfort, who had never designed a depot before, who had spent twenty years building bridges, and who, according to reports, came only occasionally to Nashville aboard his private Pullman to check out the progress, pulled off such a fine piece of work. Did he do it himself while pouring over drawings of Richardson's? Were there young draftsmen in the Louisville office who knew everything about the Romanesque style? Did he have such confidence in Major Lewis that he felt it unnessary to spend more time on site? Blueprints carry the title of his office, but no signatures or personal notes. Questions spring to mind for which there are no answers. Consequently, Montfort's credit as architect must carry with it some reservations, at least until an enlightening document emerges that either clarifies his brilliance or identifies assistants.

*The main entrance off Broad Street.*

# Building a Landmark

On August 1, 1898, ground for Union Station was broken. To level the site more than two hundred thousand cubic yards of earth were dug by hand and hauled away in wagons. More than two hundred houses and commercial buildings were razed in a fine neighborhood, making many people furious once again with the L&N and, by extension, with Major Lewis. Stonecutters and carvers, masons, carpenters, artisans, plumbers, ironsmiths, tile layers, roofers, mule handlers, and laborers were hired.

In Bowling Green, Kentucky, quarrymen mined the limestone for Union Station's walls. Called Bowling Green greystone it was oily, very uniform, and with the proper tools sliced like cheese. Large blocks traveled by rail to Nashville and there Major Lewis, seated in his buggy by the tracks, sometimes watched stone carvers chiseling geometric patterns and stonecutters making lintels, cornerstones, ashlars and the first of thousands of building blocks.

A foundation was laid and carpenters erected wooden forms. Using gin poles and derricks to hoist the stones, masons began the walls and arches at track level. The mortar between the stones was conspicuously thick. This technique gave limestone blocks a kind of flexibility and kept the joints of the arches uniform with those of the horizontal courses.

Once the masons reached the height of Broad Street, large arches encircled the entire building. When it was built later, the porte-cochère had wrought iron balustrades and stained glass beneath the eaves. A low portico, also built after most of the station was completed, bordered the Broad Street viaduct. On it large chiseled letters spelled out UNION STATION in smooth-faced limestone. The biggest arch in the building, it formed an inviting entryway for travelers arriving by trolley or on foot. Lacy wrought iron decorative work added to the appeal of this portico.

Ironsmiths wrought the iron on site for the decorative railings. These men were quick, sweaty craftsmen with strong forearms and a penchant for jokes about the fires of hell. The metal they worked was soft yet tough. Heated red-hot over coal-fired flames, then bent and twisted, drawn and spiraled, it was bolted and welded into place. This hand-forged work contrasted sharply with the cast iron columns

that supported much of the interior of the station. A relatively new building material, cast iron came preformed in rigid columns with fancy Gothic capitals. Laborers held the columns in place and they were simply bolted to the ceiling and the floor—no fire, no forging, little drama.

As derricks lifted the blocks to the masons on each succeeding floor, the upper levels of the station took shape. The rows of windows gave each side a visual pattern. Inside, around the large, central barrel vault, which meant literally half a giant barrel on its side, a combination of brick pillars and cast iron columns supported the second, third and attic floors. Walls and partitions were framed with wood. Floors were wood. The interior walls were plastered and frequently wainscoted. Bathrooms were tiled everywhere.

At the roof line tall gables marched all around the station like little castles. The roof was steeply pitched and finished with an ornamental crest line and little hooks called Viking points.

Except for the arches of stained glass that let light into the interior of the restaurant, the lunch room, and the secondary waiting rooms, all the windows in the station were clear, framed in wood, and usually double-hung so they could be raised during the hot

Top: *Timbers, limestone, nails and other materials arrived on the site by rail.*

Bottom: *Masons laid the limestone blocks with mortar. A keystone at the top of each arch completed it so the bracing could be removed.*

days of summer and quickly dropped if a sudden breeze wafted in cinders from a passing locomotive. Square transoms were placed over the tops of the second-story windows and arched transoms over the tops of the gable windows.

Two towers rose above the roof line. The rear one, whimsically supported by buttresses, functioned as a flue for the huge fireplace in the main waiting room and as a circulator for the primitive ventilation system. The front tower soared above its flanking gables and ended with an acorn on which Mercury stood on tiptoe, one arm outstretched. Major Lewis, who had salvaged the Greek god from the roof of the Commerce Building at the Centennial, had it placed on top of Union Station by W.E. Jordan, a subcontractor who recalled his dealings with the major as a little strained but worth it.

"There were several problems involved," Jordan told a reporter for the *L&N Magazine* years later, "but I was sure we could get the statue on a flat car to the viaduct and from the viaduct to the concourse by means of a derrick. After we got Mercury that far I figured we could erect a temporary platform and, working from it, eventually get the statue in its place by means of a gin pole and pulley arrangements.

Top: *Here work proceeds on the plenum, a five-foot-tall heating space beneath the floor of the main waiting room.*

Bottom: *The station with three floors completed.*

"While these plans were being formed in my head, Major Lewis became impatient—too impatient, I thought—so I decided to put him off a bit. I calculated that I could make a good profit charging one hundred dollars for the job, but the major's insistence bothered me. Each time he asked me about the thing—and that was often—I upped the price in my mind. Finally I told him I'd do the job for five hundred and he jumped at the offer."

With Mercury standing on the roof, Union Station had a style and visual energy no other building in Nashville could match. To a child the station seemed a castle, to an arriving traveler a towering mass with a statue on top, to an architect a sense of recognition that architect Richardson's spirit had worked its magic here. To all who took the time to look and really see, horizontal elements like the blocks of limestone, the arches, and the smooth stone bands demarcating the floors swept the eyes sideways. Vertical elements like the towers, the gables, the tall narrow windows, and the steep pitch of the roof swept the eyes upward. The imagination could play with Mercury or try to figure out how the digital clock worked. The primitive psyche could lean over the railing of the via-

*The station nears completion. The concourse soon butted the building above the rectangular train tunnels.*

duct and check out the alligators in the two pools at track level. All of this left a strong and lasting impression.

The shed, beneath which ten passenger trains could be sheltered, stretched behind the station like some low-profiled body attached to a raised stone head.

The shed was the largest unsupported span yet erected in America. Two hundred and fifty feet wide and five hundred feet long, it was supported by exposed steel beams that formed a picturesque network. A delight to look at (and the reason Union Station would receive National Historic Landmark status seventy-five years later), its design was far

more innovative than that of the station. The shed was an almost playful tribute to steel's strength and contrasted to the massive stone monument it served.

As for its position in relation to the station, the shed honored William Henry Vanderbilt's "public-be-damned" style. That is, in lieu of placing the loading platforms and the waiting rooms on the same level, as some designers were starting to do, Union Station stuck with the traditional scheme. Passengers in Nashville got plenty of exercise going up and down the long stairways connecting the shed to the main concourse.

Major Lewis, of course, oversaw every-

*The largest unsupported span yet erected in America, the shed was far more innovative in design than the station.*

25

thing. Daily he rode his carriage from his home on Belmont Boulevard to the construction site in "the gulch" on the edge of downtown. Being practically everywhere on the site suited his restless nature. He had bought much of the fifty-seven acres and then steered the Depot Bill around Colonel Baxter and through the city council. Making sure that every detail of the project got done right was merely following through. From his employer's point of view, Major Lewis was a godsend. From an employee's, appearing unexpectedly, always watchful, he could be a pain in the neck.

Officially, as president of the Terminal Company, Major Lewis approved plans, awarded contracts, and supervised construction. Unofficially, he promoted his private aesthetic vision. That the finished station would reflect some strange design flair might have been guessed by anyone who had visited the major's own home with its angular exterior and curved interior.

Major Lewis's fascination with ancient Greece transported Mercury to the roof of Union Station. As an admirer of the late-nineteenth-century practice of including art in public places, he insisted on bas-relief sculptures (bas-relief is sculpture in which the figures project slightly from the background) in the main waiting room. Although neither unusual nor extraordinary individually, the bas-relief work was artistic in its total effect and a fresh idea in Nashville. Most people had never seen anything quite like this.

The main waiting room left quite an impression on those entering Union Station for the first time. Waiting for trains, people climbed the stairs to the balcony that cantilevered out over the main floor and got close-up views of the angels, wings outspread and filling the spandrels of the arched entrances to the railroad offices. The balustrade was a fine place to lean. From there, one could peer down at fellow travelers buying tickets, having their shoes shined or their hair cut, or starting towards the main concourse as the gateman in his black uniform and cap called out that their train was leaving in fifteen minutes.

*The main waiting room soon after the station opened.*

On the main level in the northeast front of the station was a fancy restaurant where the food rivaled that in a dining car. It had a twenty-two-foot ceiling, rose colored walls, and floor tiles laid in geometric patterns. The ladies' waiting room, with garlands of pink roses painted on the ceiling, was in the northwest corner. A nurse assigned there assisted flustered mothers with their "lap organs," as crying children were called.

Segregation restricted blacks to the col-ored waiting room in the southwest corner. It had a decorative ceiling and large clear windows with arched transoms.

For those in a hurry or on a budget, a large lunch room complete with two horseshoe-shaped counters and booths along the wall served the turn-of-the-century equivalent of fast food. On the floor of the main waiting room wooden benches gave the weary and waiting a place to sit. A water fountain with two silver cups, one for whites and the

*The* Bully 108 *symbolized modern locomotive power.*

27

Above: *Balustrades of wrought-iron with hardwood handrails decorated both the interior and exterior.*

Opposite page: *A blueprint of finish work in the main waiting room.*

other for blacks, stood near the large fireplace whose flue rose to the buttressed rear tower.

The decorated interior was unique in Nashville. Architect Henry H. Richardson had boosted this concept of art as an integral part of original design when he had completed the Trinity Church in Boston in the 1870s. Richardson had persuaded the deacons of the church to pay artist John LaFarge to paint murals as part of the construction process, rather than as an afterthought. Presumably Major Lewis knew of the commission and of others that American artists had recently completed in both sculpture and painting in such buildings as the Library of Congress and the new state capitols in Minnesota and Rhode Island.

Although modest himself Major Lewis took advantage of this decorative trend in architecture to immortalize his daughter on Union Station's south wall. Eighteen-year-old Louise Lewis posed for J.M. Doner, the artist from Chicago who did the bas-relief work. Opposite her, stretching out a hand in greeting, was the daughter of L&N president, Milton Smith, Major Lewis's boss.

Ever since the World's Columbian Exposition of 1893 artisans from Chicago had been much sought after. Major Lewis hired a number of them. Besides Doner, who stayed in Nashville for nine months working on his commission, The Almini Company, Nelson & Brothers, and the Luminous Prism Company were also from Chicago. They did the interior painting, the interior decoration, and the stained-glass work respectively. Critiquing

Doner's bas-relief of Louise Lewis, a reporter for the *Nashville Banner* wrote that the major's daughter was: "rather undeveloped, yet . . . a promising figure. She is most becomingly draped and, thus bestowed in lavender and pink, energetically stretches out a glad hand to Louisville's worthy representative [who] is dressed all in white; the pink glow of bluegrass health and happiness and development adorns the cheeks, neck, and arms. The face is fair, the figure is superb; so is the lady."

Miss Nashville and Miss Louisville were draped in robes and their faces distorted because of the nature of bas-relief. Distortion created better definition from a distance.

Later in his article the reporter described the angels of commerce on the side walls. He wrote that the "veritable Ladies Bountiful . . . soar along, bearing to the two roads the principal products, by the transportation of which they derive their income." He listed the products the angels held in their extended hands, including whiskey, which he excused by conceding that both the L&N and the NC&St L made good profits from "the pesky stuff."

He did not comment on the exposed breast of each angel. In this era of long-sleeved gowns for tennis and fainting couches to aid the weaker-spirited ladies with the "vapors," the somewhat risque angels were a stylization; even Victorians needed some acknowledgement of the flesh.

Beneath the two young ladies on the south wall, artist Doner sculpted a plaster representation of the *1900 Limited*, a modern passenger train. The train was being pulled

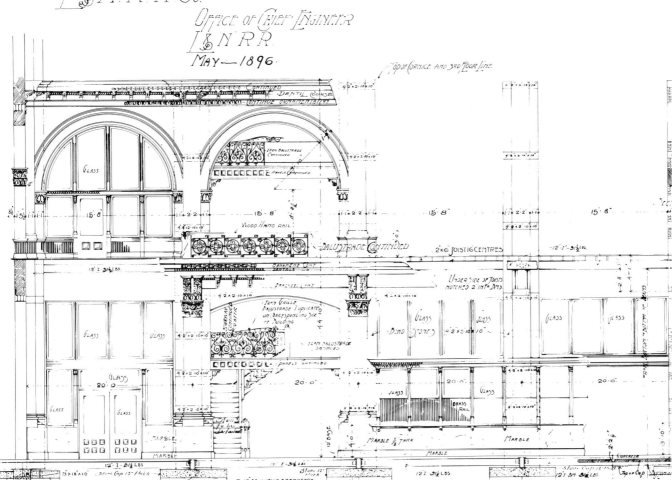

*From the left: Margaretta, Louise, Anita and Floy Lewis. Louise, age eighteen, posed for artist J.M. Doner's version of Miss Nashville (above).*

by a bully engine number 108. "Bully" in those days meant first rate, and the number 108 was exactly that. Here Doner's work had excellent proportion and fine detail on the locomotive, big wheels turning, the engineer leaning out the window in his overalls.

On the opposite wall of the main waiting room a huge clock told travelers the hour. On either side of the clock stood Time and Progress. Time spun the "thread of life." Progress, the single male among the angels, smiled as he hugged a railroad wheel to his chest.

Beneath Time and Progress an Egyptian pharaoh and his wife were being pulled along by slaves. The intent was contrast. The ancient scene reminded everyone how far civilization had come. Now instead of moving along at the pace of slaves, one could buy a ticket and get on board the *1900 Limited*.

Straight overhead, sixty-three feet from the floor, was the gem of the interior, a curved, stained-glass ceiling that lifted a trav-

eler's eyes. If the sun was high, colored shafts of light pierced the glass. The one hundred and twenty-eight panels of stained glass sat in curved wooden ribs. Because of the height-to-width ratio of the room, it was difficult, if not impossible, to appreciate this fine work by the Luminous Prism Company without craning the neck back and staring almost straight up.

Two large gaslit chandeliers hung from chains for night lighting. The ends and sides of the vault, as well as the coffers, the plaster cornice, the brackets, the frieze, and the woodwork were painted and varnished. The dominant color was green, dark green on the lower areas and a lighter shade toward the stained-glass ceiling. Yellow, mauve and gilded highlights accented the various decorative elements. Every coffer on the upper reaches of the vault had a medallion. A huge one decorated the north wall, suggesting a tremendous sunflower lifting towards colored light.

Upstairs were the interconnecting offices

*Geometric patterns made the floors as attractive to look at as the ceilings and walls.*

of the L&N and NC&St L administrative personnel. Seven built-in vaults provided storage for documents and money.

At the top of the building, unheated and poorly ventilated, was the attic, which was used for additional storage space. Stacked in one corner were two sets of replacement treads for the main staircases. Given the hardness of white oak, this was an optimistic statement from Major Lewis regarding his faith in the long-term future of Union Station, a faith the automobile would almost immediately start to challenge and by the 1970s completely run over.

Access to the stained-glass ceiling was

from the attic. There workmen could examine the laminated curved beams that formed the vault and cradled the glass. Large trusses held the walls together and a clear glass skylight overhead shielded the stained glass from the elements.

More than one hundred feet below, at track level, were the shops, locker rooms for yard men and crews, maintenance areas, and the boiler room with its giant steam tanks, valves the size of steering wheels, and sweaty black men shoveling coal. An interesting space called a plenum separated the ceiling of the basement areas from the floor of the main waiting room. Here, crouched over since it was only five feet high, metal workers had installed ducts to carry hot air to the upper offices of the station.

A final interior space, and one of the most intriguing, was the vertical shaft of the front tower. Secured to its brick interior was a wooden staircase not designed for the fainthearted. Appearing to simply dangle from the wall (in fact, it was supported by beams set in niches in the bricks), it ascended from the second floor up to the bicycle chains and linen belts of Major Lewis's digital clock that was so far ahead of its time that it couldn't keep time. Passengers were not allowed access here, but employees could climb the tower. Workmen involved in the construction also seemed to have found the shaft alluring. A number of them, using various sharp instruments, recorded their initials, names and the names of their loved ones in the wood framing of the small windows at the very top.

# Alligator Pools, A Digital Clock, and Mercury

In spite of his quirky character, dominating style, and obsession with punctuality, Major Lewis had a childish spot of large dimensions. He loved odd juxtapositions that evoked wonder and delight. He built a carnival-like set for alligators at track level. He struggled for years to get the digital clock to work in the tower. And he bought the statue of Mercury after the end of the Centennial Exposition and put it at the very top of the front tower for all of Nashville to admire. An entertaining Union Station was the consequence, a place with strong evocations of childhood about it.

In all likelihood Major Lewis got the idea for the two alligator pools at track level—trains going north on one side and south on the other—while vacationing in Florida. It was his custom to take his wife and children to Jupiter Island each winter. Caged alligators in front of Florida hotels, if not a common sight, were not that rare either.

Major James Geddes, superintendent of the Nashville Division of the L&N, actually brought the original reptiles home, and his grandson, James G. Stahlman, recalled the details.

"Mayor Geddes spent about six weeks of every winter in St. Petersburg, Florida," Stahlman said, "and on more than one occasion he would bring baby alligators back for me and my sister Mary. The alligators were about a foot to a foot and a half long and were allowed to sleep on the hearth or in the cooling ashes of the dining room grate because this was the only heat that they could get at night, and they would have died otherwise. They had to be kept warm."

In an era when the law and company policy were vague about such matters as alligator pools, Major Geddes collaborated with Major Lewis. Once the pools were finished Major Geddes could see the alligators from the window of his office, which was next to the tower on the third floor of the station.

"They were not full grown," his grandson said. "You couldn't have a full-grown alligator; . . . [it] would have been anywhere from eight to ten feet long. The ones at Union Station were very small. I don't think there was anything at the Union Station over three or four feet long, as I recall. They couldn't have kept them in a small enclosure like that, and they had to be fed regularly. I don't think too many of the help around Union Station were

33

enamored of the job of taking care of those alligators!"

The number of alligators fluctuated, depending on the cooperativeness of travelers returning from Florida. The two symmetrical pools were made of cement, filled with warm water from the boiler room, and surrounded by high fences. When the sun was hot, the reptiles crawled out of the pools and sunned on the cement aprons. Children from Nash-

*In the early 1900s, alligator pools were popular sights outside Florida hotels.*

ville who had never ridden a train in their lives loved to hang over the viaduct and watch them. Despite their small size, the alligators frightened parents, whose children often leaned so far over the railing of the viaduct that they had to collar them before they tumbled.

By 1908 the surprise and fascination of the alligators had worn thin, though, and one pool was removed. In cold weather the remaining alligators were moved inside the station to the boiler room where a large tank filled with warm water provided them with enough heat to get through the winter.

The second pool disappeared as well during World War I. Reasons included the war, which made such things seem frivolous by comparison, as well as the long-standing parental concern for the safety of their children. Stories of children attempting to scale the fence continued to circulate, and whether true or not, frightened people. One tale claimed that drunks tossed a Negro child over the fence and the alligators had to be destroyed after eating him.

By 1919 a child who wanted to see alligators at Union Station peered down at the roofs of maintenance sheds; the alligators were gone.

The Major's digital clock disappeared from the tower about the same time. This clock, which was supposed to provide everyone in Nashville with the exact time, had seldom worked quite right. It drove the aging major up and down the tower stairs until he had the thing removed, rebuilt and installed again. Even then it did not keep the same time in all four directions.

Major Lewis had had the clock built in Philadelphia for the 1900 opening. From the very beginning there were problems. Letters of reprimand from him to the clock makers regarding delays survive, and the exasperated man even traveled by train to Philadelphia to see what was hampering progress.

The design complicated matters. A digital clock in which the numbers dropped into rectangular openings was unheard of in 1899. It was a challenge to make, particularly since the rectangles in which the numbers would appear were two feet high and eight feet long.

Once the clock was installed in the tower—an unheated space subject to winds, rain and extremes of heat and cold—the problems multiplied. The clock ran on a standard weight and pendulum arrangement, but it also had sixty-nine wheels, eighty feet of shafts, one hundred feet of bicycle chain, six hundred and eighty feet of steel banding, and three hundred and forty feet of linen canvas belts specially woven in France. Maintenance men got plenty of exercise going up and down the stairs of the tower. Major Lewis went up and down the stairs more times than he cared to count. Things were always going wrong.

Late in life Major Lewis admitted in a letter to a friend that parts from the clock littered his back yard. J.W. Braid, an inventor credited with improvements on Nashville's first telephone system, frequently collaborated

with the frustrated major to get the four rectangular openings to agree on the time. A clock maker from Louisville even traveled to Nashville by train, climbed the steps of the tower, and offered advice as to how to make this veritable puzzle of gears, linen and bicycle chain work right.

Any visitor to the apparatus, once he reached the platform on which the main clockworks sat, first caught his breath. The pendulum was swinging, gears turning, shafts rotating, and bicycle chains inching along. Rising toward the rectangular openings were sets of canvas belts. There was one set of belts with large rollers for each of the four openings. The belts were painted with numbers: the belts for hours numbered one to

*Mercury achieved perfect symbolic pitch: eloquence without words.*

twelve, the belts for ten-minute intervals numbered one to five, and the belts for minutes numbered one to nine. If the visitor happened to be there on the hour, he saw twelve belts rotating if the clock was working properly, which was unlikely. The rotating belts were powered by three electric motors, one each for the minute belts, the ten-minute interval belts, and the hour belts. An arrangement of weights tripped each motor at the appropriate time.

One can imagine what a little freezing rain in February did to the belts and the difficulties caused by broken bicycle chains, snapped shafts, snagged gears, and burnt-out motors. In 1911 the indefatigable Major Lewis finally admitted, "The two hundred and ninety steps [have] got too much for me." He ordered the clock removed and sent to Louisville for modernization.

Years later, when the clock had not yet been returned and the clock maker demanded more money, Major Lewis's patience snapped like an overwound spring.

"We will all be dead directly!" he declared. He ordered the clock returned immediately.

Home again with a new self-winding mechanism and many new wheels and shafts, the clock synchronized correctly at 2:30 P.M. on Thursday, October 16, 1916. An elated Major Lewis wrote to his old friend Milton Smith in Louisville that the "long promised time indicator has at last been completed, and runs all right by day and by night, four ways to the windward."

The boast was premature. The belts, which should have been replaced when the clock was returned in 1916, were old and frayed. They began fouling up the works. Getting linen replacements from the French during World War I proved impossible. Then, to brighten their appearance, workmen painted the belts. Stiffened, they worked worse than ever.

When Major Lewis could no longer climb the tower, no employee with his zealousness for punctuality came forth to assume the burden of the digital clock. It was abandoned in 1919 and the rectangles boarded up. Parts of the clock remained in the tower for decades—the cast iron frame, a pendulum, a few weights—all blanketed by dust, soot and cinders.

Above the clockworks and the alligator pools stood the element of showmanship that best withstood the passage of time, the statue of Mercury. To many it was the most memorable detail on the station, a messenger of the gods perched on high, arm raised, ready to leap great distances. A young girl writing an essay described Mercury as a "man running to catch a train."

Major Lewis had commissioned James Baxter Hodge, a young Nashville sculptor who would later become a well-known architect in the city, to make the statue to symbolize commerce and progress for the Centennial Exposition of 1897. Hodge took specially-cast copper-bronze plates, hammered them into the desired shapes over wooden forms, and assembled the pieces with copper rivets and solder. He used no internal bracing. Neither polished nor refined, but rather a form of crude folk art intended for temporary viewing at a reasonable distance, Mercury stood on top of the portico of the Commerce Building during the Centennial and then was taken down.

Given his penchant for Greek mythology, ideals and architecture, possibly Major Lewis had the resurrection of Mercury on Union

*Major Lewis's idealized version of Mercury.*

37

Station in mind all along. The Parthenon had proven so popular with the public that Mercury, though much smaller, may have come to symbolize to him Nashville's reputation as the "Athens of the South." He bought the seventeen-foot sculpture for three hundred dollars (Hodge had been paid fifteen hundred dollars as the artist) and kept it.

*Hammered out of copper-bronze plates, Mercury added seventeen feet to the front tower.*

Undoubtedly, Major Lewis knew that in the Greek pantheon, Mercury had been called Hermes and was the son of Zeus and Maia. Homer had written about Hermes in the *Odyssey*. In that epic poem of wandering and change, Hermes carried messages and escorted the dead to Hades. Over the centuries, in his role as messenger, he gradually became the god of roads and the guardian of travelers on those roads. He was also a dream god to whom the last drink of the evening was traditionally raised as a toast. The light-hearted god had a beard and wore a tunic, a cap, and winged boots. About the fifth century B.C., his beard and tunic disappeared, and, nude and youthful, Hermes came to epitomize the athlete.

The Romans adopted Hermes, idealized him, and renamed him Mercurius.

By the nineteenth century, images of Mercurius and Hermes had wound together in the minds of successive generations of painters and sculptors. Modern renditions portrayed Mercury with wings on both his cap and his feet. He was athletic, yet carried a staff. Major Lewis himself painted a rendition of this idealized figure, although for some reason he abandoned it for the folk art piece that sculptor Hodge created.

Placing Mercury on top of Union Station was a problem, but not one that a clever subcontractor, W.E. Jordan, could not solve. A flatcar moved the statue to the viaduct and then a derrick lifted it to the concourse. A gin pole and pulleys raised the seventeen-foot statue up past the limestone, the windows, and the clock. It was not the easiest thing to handle. Once on the peak of the roof, a four-inch diameter rod went straight up through the body from the left heel to the winged cap. The rod was bolted to the framing beneath the roof.

This crudely fashioned yet powerful piece became Major Lewis's most memorable orna-ment to Union Station. It bemused, humored and inspired. There was something incongru-ous yet right about the statue. Mercury spoke with perfect symbolic pitch: eloquence with out words. Strangers and Nashvillians both loved his silhouette.

The statue remained poised on the roof long after the alligators disappeared and the

*Twisted and contorted, the statue retained the hint of a bemused smile.*

linen belts not far below frayed and lost their usefulness. A dressing-up effort in 1939, which included a coat of aluminum paint and a lamp placed in the outstretched hand, prompted a public outcry. James G. Stahlman, writing in the *Nashville Banner*, said that Mercury, once a delight, was now "the most grotesque thing in these parts."

Then, with uncanny timing, just as the public made clear its preference for automobiles over trains, Mercury snapped off his rod, bounced on the roof, and fell to the track level below on a a windy morning in March, 1952. Custis Stamp, a clerk in the superintendent's office, saw the blur go by a window and knew there was only one thing that could have fallen. He went down to the tracks and took pictures to capture the historic moment.

The limbs and body of Mercury were twisted and contorted. The face, however, retained what could only be described as a beatific, and slightly bruised, smile. He had outlasted them all—Major Lewis, the alligators, the clock, even the steam locomotives that had practically disappeared along with their cinders and plumes of black smoke.

# The City and Its Station

Often a newcomer's first memory of Nashville was of Mercury silhouetted against the sky, Union Station below. His train eased to a smoky stop beneath the shed. Carrying a suitcase, he ascended the stairs, crossed the busy waiting room, and then hesitated a moment in the portico, debating whether to walk downtown or to catch a carriage or the trolley. Sometimes this newcomer was intimidated by the trolley tracks, overhead wires, and imposing buildings lining Broad as it crested a slight rise. Other times he saw his future on the horizon, coming toward him along the macadam street that no longer required watering wagons to keep the dust down.

Heading up Broad, the newcomer might glance down at the alligators, then pass the hotels, small eating places, newsstands and bars that had displaced the pre-Union Station neighborhood. Across the street sat the brick headquarters of the NC&St L. Farther along were Christ Episcopal Church, the large Vauxhall Flats, the ornate Customs House, Hume-Fogg High School, and then once one could see the Cumberland River that snaked through the city, Nashville's largest gathering hall, the Union Tabernacle.

The tabernacle was a barn-like, cavernous building. It could hold as many as six thousand people in its curved wooden pews, and housed revival meetings, suffragette conventions, political rallies, plays and a dozen other things. Built by steamboat captain Tom Ryman in the 1880s after the fiery evangelist Sam P. Jones converted the captain at a tent meeting, the tabernacle anchored a rowdy, colorful neighborhood where saloons, gambling parlors, stores and boarding houses catered to the lower classes, including the riverboat crews whose days Union Station was rapidly bringing to an end. After Captain Ryman's death in 1904 the tabernacle was renamed Ryman Auditorium. Much later in the century, when many newcomers would arrive in Nashville with guitars slung over their shoulders, it would become the home of the Grand Ole Opry.

During the early 1900s Union Tabernacle anchored one half of downtown, and the Capitol, a monumental Greek Revival building on a knoll a half mile away, anchored the other half. In the grid of streets separating the tabernacle from the Capitol was the commercial center of Nashville. Here were the banks,

*Smoke, cinder showers, and a silhouette greeted travelers arriving in Nashville.*

42

better stores, offices and professional buildings of the young city. Here in 1903, the
Arcade appeared, fifty-two shops beneath a
glass roof, the forerunner by a half century of
the shopping mall. In 1904, at the corner of
Union and Fourth, rose the city's first sky-
scraper, the twelve-story First National Bank.

It was to these streets that businessmen
rode to work aboard trolley cars each morning
from the new suburbs. Some of these men
had been raised in these very streets as boys,
when this area had housed Nashville's elite in
fine brick and wooden mansions, with trees
shading their fences.

In those years Nashville's shape had been
that of a nineteenth-century town. Commerce
had been centered at the Public Square near
the river where retail and wholesale establish-
ments thrived and proprietors often lived
with their families above their stores. Riverboat captains boarded in the same rooming
houses as revivalist preachers, and the well-
to-do lived in their neighborhoods centered
by Church and Cherry (now Fourth Avenue)
streets. Then in the mid-1890s the new street-
car systems radiating from downtown made
the suburbs an option. Many families moved.
The Centennial and Union Station propelled
Nashville into the new century and hastened
the exodus of the upper and middle classes
from downtown. Commerce moved into the
residential neighborhoods, warehouses ex-
panded in the Public Square area, and the
shape of Nashville, that of a compact, colorful
mixture of people living close together,

changed to that of a city with divisions deter-
mined by wealth, class and color.

Contrasts between the rich and the poor,
between the respectable and the derelict,
sharpened in the new century. Physical sepa-
ration fostered racial prejudice. Blacks, Irish
and other minorities lived in dismal warrens

*In 1905 a traveler could walk up Broad,
take a horse-drawn carriage, or climb aboard
the trolley for a nickel.*

of makeshift houses on the far side of the Capitol, along the riverfront, and in the gulch near Union Station. The worst of these neighborhoods carried nicknames like "Hell's Half Acre" and "Black Bottom."

A number of emotional issues buffeted the city: suffrage, temperance, segregation. Yet buoyed by a strong economy and boosted by a busy Union Station, the mood was optimistic. This was the twilight of the Gilded Era, that time in American history when optimism in the future of mankind peaked. People put great faith in science, business and transportation. In this dynamic atmosphere, entrepreneurs flourished like seeds in a hot house.

Joel Owlsley Cheek, who had ridden the Tennessee countryside during the 1880s selling green coffee beans from his saddlebags, was making Maxwell House coffee a household word in America. Andrew Mizell Burton, who had walked to Nashville with his cow and then dug ditches for a dollar a day at the Centennial, was starting Life and Casualty Insurance Corporation. H. G. Hill, who would eventually own five hundred stores throughout the South, was introducing cash-and-carry discounts in failed grocery stores that he bought at auctions. James C. Napier, who had been run out of Nashville as a boy because schools for blacks were against the law, was helping the One Cent Savings Bank get started. These men and others like them were joining the ranks of Major Lewis, now chairman of the board of the NC&St L, and others as the power brokers of twentieth-century Nashville.

These entrepreneurs based their power not on land, as their predecessors had in the ante-bellum South, but on capital, ideas and the railroads—mainstays of the Industrial Revolution. They had lobbied for Union Station's construction and now relied on the railroad to transport their goods and extend their services. They depended on the Western Union office at the station for fast communications. They often walked beneath the vaulted ceiling, dined in the fancy restaurant, descended the stairs, boarded Pullmans, and departed on business and pleasure.

The revitalized Nashville they symbolized boomed. Opportunities were plentiful. Wholesalers left the riverside area and relocated in the new Cummins Station, a huge warehouse just south of the shed. Cheek-Neal Coffee Company roasted beans there, and if the wind was right, the smell of blended Brazilian suffused passenger cars. Every day mills processed the equivalent of a trainload of wheat into five thousand barrels of flour. Shoes were made, books published, foods processed, furniture manufactured, lumber milled—then all were freighted out.

One sour note concerned the failure of the Tennessee Central. Major Lewis had left the conflict behind once the bond initiative of Colonel Baxter and Mayor Head, which they had initiated in 1900, became bogged down in lawsuits that challenged Nashville's part in their plans. The Tennessee Central came to a standstill and Colonel Baxter's efforts got more desperate. In 1903 he alienated even his staunchest supporters when he tried to get the state legislature to regulate all the railroads. Shortly after, he resigned as head of the Tennessee Central Railroad and died a year later.

Most tales were more positive, however, and many were heard along a block of Fourth Avenue called "The Men's Quarter." A woman who prized her reputation avoided

Opposite page: *A turn-of-the-century poster illustrates the importance of Union Station to Nashville commerce.*

Below: *Union Station and the shed at night.*

UNION STATION

this block. Saloons and gambling parlors fancier than those on Lower Broad enticed businessmen inside. In the famous Southern Turf, twenty-five cents bought two glasses of whiskey while ham, deviled eggs, fried oysters, cheese and other foods were free. The floor above the dining room was reserved for gambling. Nearby, Nashville businessmen negotiated with their counterparts from other cities in the Utopia and the Maxwell House hotels and assured their wives when they returned to the suburbs at night that the unsavory reputation of the latter hotel was entirely undeserved. The wives disagreed, and eventually the Maxwell House gave ladies a private entrance around the corner off Church Street.

This youthful, dynamic, growing city offered newcomers and visitors alike a host of contradictions. Victorian morality prevailed, yet prostitutes were numerous. In the saloons, streets and suburbs one found both praise and condemnation of gambling, bourbon, segregation, the Lord, suffrage and automobiles, which, among the affluent were replacing horse racing as a favorite pastime.

Oldsmobile runabouts established themselves as the sportsman's model. Service occurred alongside the road or in a local bicycle

*"The Men's Quarter" on Cherry Street (now Fourth Avenue) where saloons enticed businessmen with nickel beers and a free lunch.*

shop. Liverymen, who had been trying to convince themselves that neither the bicycle nor the car were real threats, that a man still needed a horse, continued to go out of business. Women dressing for rides in runabouts faced a dilemma. *Chat*, a society weekly, advised them to take up these new machines, but elegant hats proved difficult to keep on and dresses rippled all over. Nevertheless, the adventurous laid aside their dignity, kept one hand on the hat and another on the dress, and tried it.

A few of the men, tired of riding trolleys, cranked their engines over each morning and became Nashville's first commuters. Coming from the western suburbs, most of them drove over the viaduct in front of Union Station.

In good weather the ride was sporty and exciting. On chilly winter days the scene could become a ghostly apparition, Union Station looming like a giant overlord in the grit made of congealed smoke, soot and cinders all held aloft by the right temperature. Drivers placed scarves over their nostrils and mouths and tugged down their goggles. They learned to endure it. In the early twentieth century this was not called pollution, it was

*In 1903 the Arcade opened between Fourth and Fifth avenues in the heart of Nashville's commercial district.*

*Cavernous and nondenominational, the Union Tabernacle was renamed Ryman Auditorium in 1904. Nashville's largest assembly hall, it hosted such notables as William Jennings Bryan, Carrie Nation, Enrico Caruso,*

48

*Sarah Bernhardt, Charlie Chaplin, and, beginning in 1941, when WSM started broadcasting the Grand Ole Opry from its stage, dozens of country music stars.*

progress. A little smoke and grime seemed a small price to pay for all that Union Station and the railroad had done to improve incomes and lifestyles. Besides, much of the smoke rose from that area of the gulch where the poor heated their homes with the same soft coal the locomotives burned. The railroad was only part of it.

In 1904, promoted by the business community, Nashville adopted new street names despite opposition from the Old Guard, some of whom still lived on High, Vine and Spruce Streets, which became Sixth, Seventh and Eighth avenues respectively.

The new businessmen understood how to use a relatively new medium, advertising, to increase sales. Retail merchants banded together regularly and offered low-cost fares aboard the local trains so that country people could afford to come to town and shop.

These were people who burned candles and lamps at night and whose social contacts consisted mainly of church and the family. They boarded the train in a town or at a flag stop, arrived at Union Station, and walked around downtown looking at new styles, telephones, phonographs, automobiles and a thousand other things that had not existed a few years before. Shopping was exciting. All this machine-made materialism was new. And goods were not cheap in a time when a dollar a day was a decent wage. A suit cost fifteen dollars, shoes two dollars and a half. A shirt cost fifty cents. A fifth of Jack Daniels could be lugged back to the station for eighty cents or a bushel of potatoes for half that.

# The Only Way to Travel

The local trains that country people rode in and out of Union Station were called "accommodations." One or more accommodations ran daily to Murfreesboro, Dickson, Lebanon and other towns within an hour's distance. The railroad made riding easy. They established "flag stops" where a single passenger could wave down the Tullahoma accommodation, for example, and climb aboard. These accommodations were not very plush. They lacked dining cars and Pullmans. Passengers sat on hard wooden seats, smoke coming through the open windows in the summer, huge blocks of ice beneath the floors providing a primitive form of air conditionning. Aboard these accommodations the passengers often carried lunches in shoe boxes. Fried chicken, deviled eggs, cake and sweets were favored because they withstood the heat. Mothers usually draped aprons over their children's necks before letting them eat.

A conductor made his way down the aisle, punching tickets and collecting money. Sellers of souvenirs and fruit, called "butcher boys," hawked their wares from baskets slung over their shoulders. Colorful glass locomotives, cowboy boots, and pistols, all packed with jelly beans and candies, were part of a butcher boy's stock in trade. Frequently chewing on fried chicken, the average boy ached for one of the glass mementos filled with sweets and hoped someday, somehow, he too could be a butcher boy on an accommodation.

Long distance travel to and from Union Station was more plush. Overnight trains included comfortable coaches, Pullman sleepers, dining cars, and a lounge car. From Nashville a traveler could go almost anywhere in the country: south to Chattanooga or Miami, north to Louisville or Chicago, west to San Francisco, or east to New York. Overseas connections were made via steamship lines: the Sierra Line to Liverpool, the Teutonic Line to Bremen, the South Africa S.S. Line to Capetown, the Munson Line to Havana. On these longer trips an aura of romance and adventure prevailed. Service was excellent, the food delicious, the views memorable, and the speeds extraordinary.

Such trips demanded serious preparation. Families packed trunks with suits for the men, gowns and hats for the ladies, and

49

Below: *The* Dixie Flyer *leaves Union Station in the 1920s.*

Opposite Page: *Map from the* Local Time Tables of the Louisville and Nashville Railroad *in 1907. Connections allowed a traveler to go just about anywhere in America  or overseas via a steamship line.*

changes of clothing for the children. Arriving at the station beneath the porte-cochere, the family's carriage or automobile was unloaded by redcaps. Trunks and suitcases were tagged and wheeled on handcarts to the baggage elevator. Grips that contained items the family wanted aboard the train went with them into the station. The man of the family bought tickets that were up to two feet long (each connecting line tore its stub from the whole), and checked the departure time of the train on the trip board. Despite bragged-about efficiency, trains frequently ran late.

The gateman announced the train and track number fifteen minutes prior to departure. If friends had accompanied the travelers to see them off, there was much kissing and hugging, waving of hankerchiefs, and promises to write. For the elderly and infirm, getting to the train could be a chore because of all the stairs between the main concourse and the trains.

Several huge black locomotives might be idling impatiently at the heads of trains parked beneath the vast roof. These iron monsters seemed ill at ease when idling. Others were being switched from the adjoining yard to the fronts of trains. Firemen tried to keep the smoke coming from the stacks to a minimum, but it all too often suffused the air, making passengers eager to board. If it was evening, long cones of yellow light fell from bulbs high over the cement walkways, spotlighting smoky scenes of porters placing little metal steps by coaches and Pullmans, of last-minute embraces and goodbyes, of redcaps wheeling noisy carts piled high with trunks, suitcases and hat boxes toward the baggage car. Negroes walked toward the front of the train where the colored passenger car was attached.

Inside, porters helped Pullman passengers find their numbered berths or drawing rooms (several berths and a bath in a single compact compartment). Grips were stowed overhead. Children pressed their foreheads to the windows. The conductor cried "All aboard!" and the train eased out from beneath Union Station's shed, the engineer

giving the steam engine some throttle, the fireman shoveling on coal. Passengers on limited budgets often got their shoe boxes down before the yards were left behind; few things in life seemed to stoke the appetite as much as traveling on a train.

At certain times of the year there were grand send-offs, such as when Mary Stahlman left for college in Virginia in 1912. On the concourse girls and their well-wishers were hugging and kissing, almost all of them crying except for Stahlman who said that she was too excited about going off to school. Pullman after Pullman filled with college girls. "Our skirts were down to our ankles," she recalled, "and we wore high button-up shoes and hats. I remember my first hat had a whole pheasant on the side. A turned-up brim with a pheasant and a long coat, the top coat to your suit, almost to your knees. And this long skirt, this drab-looking thing. . . . Pictures of us looked perfectly awful."

She did not say if she packed a damp sponge to put over her nose and mouth when passing through a tunnel. A sponge kept cinders and soot out, a healthy precaution in a time when tuberculosis annually afflicted thousands.

Once the *flyer* or *special* or *limited* was clicking along the rails, many passengers looked forward to eating in the dining car. Elegant, staffed by black waiters, and with sterling silverware, fine china, and white linen on the tables, this restaurant on wheels was part of the romance of train travel. Varnished wood interiors and plush velvet seats

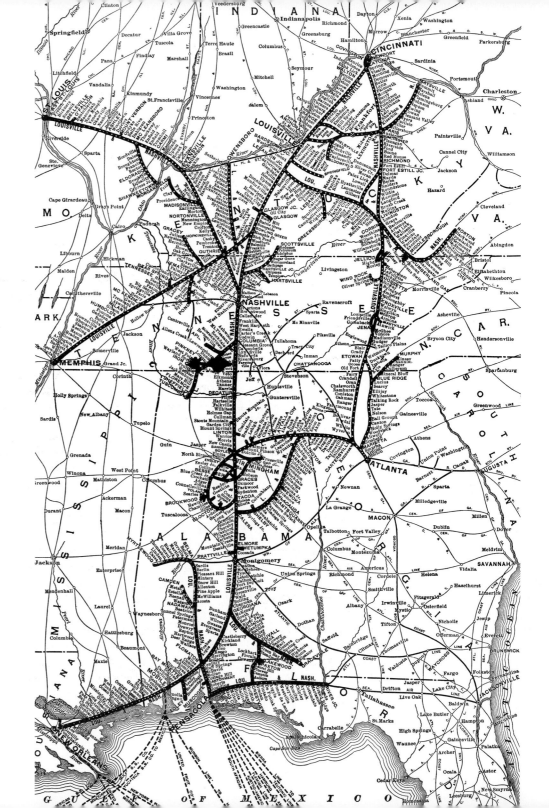

*The jacket of the 1907 Time Table shown on the previous page.*

L&N

Local
Time
Tables

Louisville
and
Nashville
Railroad

September 1, 1907. No. 153.

The Company reserves the right to vary from
the time shown in this Folder without notice to
the public and does not guarantee schedules.

added to the feeling of mobile extravagance. A steward saw to it that everything, from the flowers in the cut glass vases to the portions for children, were just right. The reputation of the dining car on the *Dixie Flyer* was so good that people from Nashville were known to board it at Union Station, travel to Chattanooga where they stayed overnight, and then return to Nashville the next day just so they could eat the food and enjoy the service.

A steward and chef managed the dining car but both of them and the rest of the train crew were under the supervision of the conductor. This man, who ranked just below the engineer in his ability to stir the imaginations of small boys, wore a black cap, a jacket and a vest, and was constantly on the go, making his way through the coaches and Pullmans, clicking tickets with his punch, making conversation, and calling out stops. His most important tool was his watch, which hung on a chain and nestled in his vest pocket. Frequently he pulled it out, flipped down the face, and checked the time.

Typically the conductor worked from a table set up in one of the passenger coaches. When numerous Pullmans made up the train, he was especially busy. In addition to his regular duties of checking tickets and announcing stops, he had to make certain the porters did their jobs, as well as handle little things that came up, like taking a look at a seat that refused to recline or catching a cat some college student had sneaked aboard in his raccoon coat.

In the hierarchy of a moving train the

Pullman porters ranked after the conductor, both in neat appearance and in passenger duties. Traditionally black men, the porters helped passengers find their berths. They stored their grips, small suitcases, and an occasional shoe box. To first-time travelers the porters might explain the call buttons in a sleeper or the method for converting berths in a drawing room into a daytime sofa. At bedtime they folded down sheets, distributed extra pillows, brought iced or hot beverages. They also kept other passengers out of the Pullmans as the train clicked and swayed through the night. One frequent challenge was the loud snorer. In the single berths, which had curtains separating them from the aisle, light sleepers had to be placated or else loud snorers tactfully tapped on the shoulder.

The thorough and gracious service offered train passengers was extraordinary yet standard during the heyday of the railroad. The first decades of the twentieth century were a time of great personal pride in service. Random, senseless crime had yet to infuse travel with an edge of paranoia. Redcaps wheeled trunks to baggage cars without having to pass bomb checks. Travel time from one place to another was longer, but the travel itself included elements of politeness and pleasure now as distant from most commercial transportation as butcher boys are from the aisles of 747s.

An anecdote told by Martha Lindsey suggested the dimensions of graciousness and concern that thrived in the railroad era.

"As we got into the car, we saw to our horror that she [a friend who had just caught a train at Union Station] had not taken her baggage. She was in 'full evening dress,' as the saying went then, so something had to be done. We decided to rush out to Bellevue and try to stop the train there. "We did make it just as the headlights came into view. All four of us—the men waving their white evening scarfs, I waving my velvet cape, took our place alongside the tracks. The train thundered past, then we noticed it had begun to

*The main waiting room on a quiet night.*

slow up. We ran down the tracks, the young men carrying the luggage, and sure enough the train did come to a stop. The conductor emerged and said, 'Where do you want to go?' When I replied that we only wanted to get the luggage to a friend on the train, he said, 'Oh, I know all about that, she is worried to death,' and took the luggage to my friend."

The *Georgian*, the *Dixie Flyer*, the *Southwind*, the *Azalea*, the *Hummingbird*—these were a few of the trains that left Union Station over the decades, their names like incantations of sumptuous and adventurous delight. Most of the travelers loved the sense of freedom, the camaraderie, the click of the tracks, the passing silhouettes of unknown towns in the night.

The atmosphere of a passenger coach was a perfect place for a storyteller to enthrall a small and captive audience. Many a child fought against dozing off as a father, grandfather, or uncle took advantage of this unparalleled situation to spin wonderful, scary or incredible tales. One of the most popular was the story of the infamous Railroad Bill, a legendary desperado who once had terrorized the lines of the L&N in Alabama. This black outlaw, whose true name was Morris Slator, carried a rifle and two pistols. He robbed freight trains by getting on board as the locomotive chugged slowly up a grade. He scampered along the swaying boxcars, tied a rope to the walkway on top, and lowered himself to a door. Railroad Bill tossed the goods off, followed himself with a bounce and a roll,

then gathered his bounty and disappeared. It was claimed that he gave much of what he had stolen to poor black families. Nicknamed for the legislative papers that attempted to regulate the railroads in the 1890s, Railroad Bill killed a number of lawmen who took his capture as a personal challenge, including one black detective who first befriended him. Railroad Bill became an Alabama folk hero. Legend claimed he could change into an animal at night and that only a silver bullet could kill him. However, a storekeeper put an end to the legend. While the hero was eating crackers and cheese on the porch of his store, the man shot him in the back. An undertaker displayed Bill's body in Montgomery, charging fifty cents for a look.

A storyteller familiar with the Nashville history of the L&N might describe Major Lewis's years of conflict with Colonel Jere Baxter and the Tennessee Central. Should the audience include teenage boys eager to test their mettle against the world, the storyteller could again draw on Major Lewis and tell about the time the major, as a boy of seventeen, had avoided becoming a prisoner during the War Between the States.

Young Eugene Lewis had been living with his parents in Clarksville when Union troops captured Fort Donelson in 1862. The boy's father, who managed the huge Cumberland Iron Works, had been forced to watch the iron works shelled by a gunboat on which he was held prisoner. Angry, disturbed and convinced he must do something, Eugene rode from his pillared mansion to where the

Union troops were bivouacked and asked a lot of questions. A Union captain became suspicious and paid a visit to Eugene's mother. He issued her an ultimatum: send that boy north to school or else he's going to a prisoner-of-war camp.

Eugene went north. In fact, it was there at the Pennsylvania Military Academy, that he aquired the title "major" by being the top cadet in his class. Major E.C. Lewis, who also graduated valedictorian of the class, never served a day in the military.

Often as not, of course, the storyteller on the train described someone in his own family or in the family of his listeners, for nearly everyone had a relative who worked on the railroad. In 1920 the railroads employed more than two million Americans, one out of every twenty-eight people between the ages of twenty and sixty-five. Like airplanes and computers in the modern day, the railroad permeated all aspects of life. It enriched the language; it was grist for stories and for songs about lonesome travelers, broken hearts, he-roic men, and terrible wrecks.

Tales about disasters always brought a listener to the edge of his seat. One infamous one occurred in 1831 during the infancy of the American railroads. On that train of the Mohawk and Hudson Railroad, the primitive cars were built from stagecoach bodies and hooked together by chains; passengers jerked backwards when the train started, then went flying forward when it attempted to stop. Pitch pine fueled the locomotive and a dense black cloud of smoke identified its progress

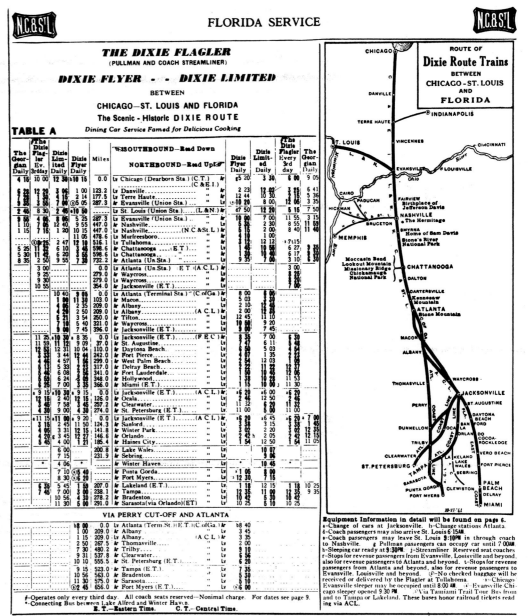

for miles around. Passengers on top of the converted stagecoaches protected themselves from flying sparks with umbrellas, but these soon caught on fire. The huge sparks then ignited clothes. The adventurous travelers beat out the flames on each other. Meanwhile, hundreds of curious spectators flocked to the tracks to witness this history-making day. The belching locomotive and scorched passengers combined to terrify the spectators' horses who took immediate flight. Carriages were strewn all over.

A mournful and modern tale, one that a traveler might have heard sung as a ballad, was about one of America's great folk heroes who died in a crash the morning of April 30, 1900, when his passenger train, the *Cannon-ball Express*, plowed into the rear of a freight train near Vaughan, Mississippi. Casey Jones, a native of Jackson, Tennessee, was tall, hand-some, on the reckless side, and had perfected a distinctive whippoorwill whistle so folks would know when his engine was hurtling down the tracks. However, on the night of his last run he was substituting for a sick engineer and started from Memphis ninety-five minutes late. Casey vowed to "pull her in on time" and had made up eighty-five minutes when he rounded a corner and saw part of a disabled freight train on his track. Casey yelled to his black fireman to jump, which he did, saving his life. Casey remained at the throttle and slowed his train enough so that no passengers were seriously injured.

"Casey Jones, the Brave Engineer," spawned other songs about trains, engineers and wrecks, like the "Wabash Cannonball," "Midnight Special," and "The Wreck of the Old 97." It was a fortunate traveler who heard these songs sung to the sound of a guitar and the click of steel.

Closer to home, Union Station had its own grisly tale. On July 9, 1918, two trains collided head-on only a mile out of Nashville. More than one hundred people died, most of them Negroes returning from work at the powder mill in Old Hickory, and twice that number were injured. James McCanless described the crash like this: "Those two trains had run together, and those locomotives had reared up just like two bulldogs fighting. . . . There was a lot of black people on those cars going home from the powder plant. . . . They were so thick in the cars they was standing in the aisles, there wasn't no seating for all of them. When those cars telescoped, it caught them in there and just killed them like sheep."

The accident happened because the engineer driving the train out of Union Station mistook a switching engine and its cars for the train that was supposed to be arriving, failed to consult with the conductor, and pulled out into the path of the oncoming train.

There were good times as well, many more than the few bad ones. Yet the disasters captured headlines. They etched their details in people's hearts as well as in their memories. One such horror accompanied the influenza epidemic that killed thousands during World War I. Coffins stacked three high

*Veterans of the Thirtieth Division arrive home after World War I.*

57

stretched down the shed walkways between arriving and departing trains. The lines of caskets were an eerie, unnerving sight in an extremely hectic place.

Thousands of young men were mobilized during World War I and passed through Union Station on their way to train and to fight. Intense, emotional partings occurred continuously. Out in the shops, dozens of passenger coaches were converted into troop carriers. Civilian travel was drastically curtailed. The wartime director of railroads issued an order that any employee found contributing to an unnecessary delay of a military train would be terminated. People working at the station had to keep on their toes. Ticket clerks and yard men worked twelve-hour shifts, seven days a week, for months on end.

During the war one of the busiest lines ran out to the Old Hickory powder plant.

Once America entered the fight in 1917, the munitions plant needed thousands of additional workers. Some came from as far away as Memphis. Trains from Union Station carried workers to and from the plant morning, noon and night.

A famous post-Armistice event at the station was the return of the Thirtieth Division. Thousands of Nashvillians, including dozens of Union Station employees who crowded together in the windows of their offices, watched the veterans parade along Broad Street while horns blew, flags waved, and bands played.

Another noteworthy event of 1919 was the death of Major Lewis. The NC&St L stopped all the trains on its lines for five minutes as a tribute to him. He was buried in Mount Olivet Cemetery overlooking the city he had affected so much. His tombstone is a pyramid guarded by two sphinxes.

# Working There

Granddaddy was an engineer on the L&N. . . . Sometimes Grandmother and I would stand on a wooden platform next to the tracks to wait for his train. . . . I would blow this silver horn to welcome him home. He would throw out his big lunch basket and my grandmother would catch the basket by its handle with her right hand and blow Grandpa a kiss with her left. Sometimes the basket was filled with flowers that would scatter as he threw it.

—Thelma Petty, *Speaking of Union Station*

From such images as those of Thelma Petty emerged the romantic folklore of working on the railroad. It was a time when firemen returned home to tell how they had cooked eggs and bacon on shovels in the firebox, a time when lonely women thought they recognized the whistle of their lover's train on every passing freight in the night. There were no televisions and no interstates. An airport was a mowed hayfield where crazy aviators put down. Railroads were supreme and they pervaded the American psyche, imagination and song. The railroad was the life of tens of thousands of families and touched nearly everyone. The visual embodiment of that touching in every town and city was the railroad station and the tracks running beside it. Working there meant one was part of something special.

In Union Station, from the lowliest coal shoveler in the boiler room to the most fastidious clerk in the superintendent's office on the third floor, employees shared this sense. There was something different about working for the railroad, a feeling of being part of something so big and enchanting that it had created its own legends like Railroad Bill, Casey Jones, and spike-driving John Henry, its own insatiable capitalists like Jay Gould and William Henry Vanderbilt, and its own ribbon of steel punctuated by hundreds of colossal architectural statements like Union Station. Of course, it didn't hurt that the pay was good and that after several years a worker received free passes. A rigid seniority system also made railroad jobs exceptionally secure.

People in Nashville were proud to work for the L&N and the NC&St L. Few ever quit. In fact, many put in forty or fifty years until they, as the lingo put it, "fell in the harness."

Jobs inside the station, for the most part, were less romantic than those on the road, although a certain allure went with being one of the four Union Station "dicks," or detectives. Nevertheless, the grand building inspired a sense of camaraderie. One was just on a lower rung of railroad romance and after work it was home to bed instead of to a caboose.

A young man starting work at the station or in the yards went through a period of on-the-job training without pay. Called "cubbing," this training typically lasted six to eight weeks or until a supervisor thought the cub was ready to join the payroll. In 1912, for instance, starting pay for a job greasing bearings in the locomotive repair shop was seven and one-half cents an hour, for a ten-hour day, with no coffee breaks and no cigarette smoking.

In both Union Station and the yards a cub soon picked up the language. In addition to his trainee name, he learned that a "trick" was a working shift and that when an engineer said he had "cleaned a slate," he meant he had stopped his train for an emergency. "Fell in the harness" was a phrase brought along by farmers abandoning the plow.

To the ears of many young farmers, train whistles played an irresistible tune. One consequence was that Union Station and many other depots, at least until World War II, had a large number of employees who had recently left the land. As might have been expected, these people formed closely-knit groups that socialized and attended church together. They shared the same worries and rumors, the same piles of smoky overalls if the man of the house worked in the yards and the same soot-collared white shirts if he was a clerk inside the station.

Generations of a family often succeeded each other at the same job or worked in the

*A yardman scales a boxcar for "The Old Reliable" L&N Railroad.*

60

same branch of railroad operations. A network of characters with colorful names like Tootsie Fleming, Friday Watts, and Hogshead Davis were part of their lives. The NC&St L was even nicknamed "kinfolks road."

In this network blacks held the lowest and toughest jobs. Railroad Bill may have cowered the great L&N and John Henry have driven spikes like a machine, but less legendary blacks emptied red-hot coals from the bellies of locomotives, shoveled fresh coal in to take its place, and pushed brooms around the tile floor of the main waiting room and between the wooden benches on which they were not allowed to sit. Being a redcap was one of the better jobs for a black man. The luckiest of those got "rolled over" to mail handler and lugged sacks of mail from the postal cars. Some thought the best jobs were in the fancy restaurant, where both cooks and waiters were black. The most responsible position, which kept a black man constantly on the rails, was as a Pullman porter.

Despite his position on the train, when the porter decided to take advantage of his free passes, he waited for his train at Union Station in the colored waiting room. If he was thirsty he filled the colored person's silver cup at the fountain in front of the fireplace and glanced at the white folks on the benches, some of whom he might even know from having made up their beds. He rode to his destination in the colored passenger car. Segregation was the law.

Women were seldom hired at all, as most jobs were considered unfit for a lady and rail-road policy was simply to ignore them. In Union Station the stenographers, secretaries and clerical workers were all men until World War II, when a shortage of able-bodied males forced the railroad to change its hiring strat-

*Travelers listen to ticket agent H.W. Loftin explain their "to California" tickets. Each connecting line tore its stub off the two-foot tickets. On the trip board the boys could check their departure time from Nashville.*

egy. Therefore, when it was said that railroading was "in the blood," it was in male blood, at least until World War II. Women provided the support system.

In Nashville many railroad families lived south of Broad Street between Third and Fifth avenues. Railroad personnel in operations—engineers, brakemen, flagmen, conductors and porters—were always on call. When the phone rang, they had an hour and a half to be down at the station.

A total of about twenty-five hundred employees worked for the L&N and the NC&St L in and around Nashville in the 1920s, with four to five hundred of these in Union Station itself. Tracks adjacent the station handled the switching demands and some repairs. Several miles away, at Thirty-first and Charlotte avenues, were the "new shops." Here the L&N had built a round-house for turning locomotives and had consolidated facilities that had been scattered all over Nashville in the pre-Union Station years.

Hundreds of men worked in the new shops. Using old equipment, switchmen hauled locomotives that had been taken off trains passing through Union Station to these shops for repair and maintenance. When one was worn, they rebuilt it using huge wrenches and tools that seemed more appropriately designed for Paul Bunyan. If there was one thing about steam locomotives that everyone remembered, it was their sheer size. This was not technology; this was might.

There was a special shed for repairing the seats, doors, wheels, drafty windows, loose couplings, brake hoses, and other worn parts of passenger, Pullman and freight cars, as well as parts sheds and sidings and junk heaps where few of the abandoned pieces weighed less than a hundred pounds. Watering towers stood in the air and coal bins hugged blackened ground. Storerooms filled with lanterns, picks and spikes were near crisscrossed stacks of creosote-smelling ties and shiny piles of rails.

Inside Union Station was a light-repair shop for passenger trains passing through. Two "car men" checked brakes and inspected steam connections and hook-ups for broken hoses. An electrician and a machinist handled minor power failures and mechanical problems.

Just north of the station on Tenth Avenue were the freight warehouses. More than a block long, these brick warehouses handled goods shipped to Nashville. Horse-drawn drays, and later trucks, backed up to the street side to load the goods that freight cars had unloaded on the track side.

Even Radnor Lake was part of Union Station's broad Nashville geography, supplying fresh water to the steam locomotives. The tanks on a locomotive might hold fifteen thousand gallons, but that water did not last very long. Frequent stops en route were necessary to top up the tanks.

Radnor Lake proved not only a good source of water but a money saver as well—it eliminated the need to buy water from the city of Nashville. It also provided the station with its annual Christmas tree, which typically stood about thirty feet. Early December each year, saws in hand, several men from the yards went out to the lake, stalked the surrounding basin, and dropped a well-proportioned fir or cedar.

In 1922 W.A. Anderton's father-in-law, who was a conductor, talked the recently married farmer into joining the exodus from the land to work for the railroad. Anderton left his farm in Bell Buckle and became one of twenty-two mail handlers who worked around the clock at Union Station, nine each on the two main shifts or "tricks," and four on split shifts.

Union Station was still "a mighty big place to me," Anderton recalled. "Locomotives come through there puffin' and blowin'."

The fireman was supposed to wait until the train pulled out from beneath the shed before throwing fresh coal on the fire, because when the fire was built up, smoke spewed out the steam locomotive's stack, causing a cinder shower.

More than two dozen long-distance passenger trains passed through daily when Anderton went to work beneath the shed. There were local accommodations morning, noon, late afternoon, and night. They all had a postal car, as did the freight trains, and Anderton helped unload plenty of them. He was paid two dollars a day for ten hours' labor, a workday markedly shorter than he had been used to on the farm. He also worked only six days a week.

All the passenger trains stopped on one of the ten sets of tracks housed beneath the shed roof. Southbound trains arrived along tracks three, four and five, which were on the east side of the shed. Northbound trains were on tracks ten, eleven and twelve on the west side. Tracks six, seven, eight and nine, which

*The ticket counter in 1942.*

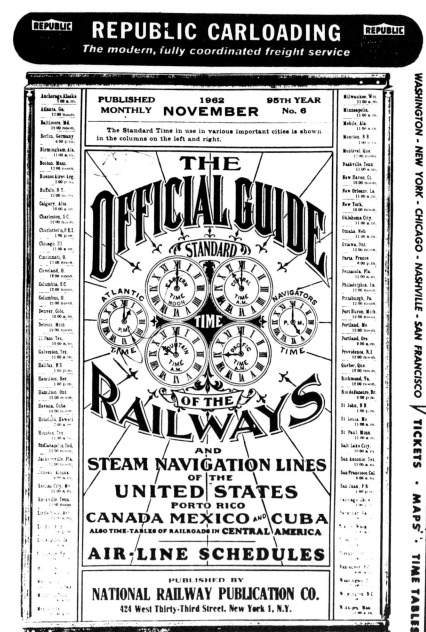

were between, butted the cement walkway near the base of the stairs; these tracks were only long enough for seven or eight cars to be parked so that passengers could be loaded and unloaded. Tracks numbered thirteen and up were outside the shed, toward Kayne Avenue; they handled the freight trains.

Anderton remembered the shed as being hot, smoky and hectic in the summer, and cold, smoky and hectic in the winter. When the temperature dropped, "the wind would eat you up." A snow storm could make a train run four or five hours late. It arrived smothered in white, black smoke billowing out its stack and passengers rubbing at moisture on their windows for a peek out.

A standard passenger train consisted of a locomotive and a coal car, a postal car, a baggage car, six to eight passenger cars and/or Pullmans, depending on the destination, a smoker and/or dining car, and a passenger car for colored people. The crew was made up of the engineer, the fireman, the conductor, the porters, the crew of the dining car, and the flagman. Once the train stopped, the flagman hung a red lantern on the rear of the last car to warn any approaching train that this track was occupied. Then the flagman peered down the side of the cars towards the conductor who motioned him to open the air brake if the train needed to back up a little. If the conductor wanted the train to ease forward a little for better positioning, he signaled the engineer to pull out a little on the throttle.

Once the conductor was satisfied, the porters placed their metal stools by the stairs of the cars. The passengers alighted. Redcaps loaded and unloaded trunks and baggage. Mail handlers hauled mail sacks to and from the postal car. Friends and family shifted in and out of the way, trying to spot whomever they were waiting for.

At the head of the train, a switching crew attended to the uncoupling of the locomotive and coal car, pulled them off onto a spur, and coupled on a fresh locomotive and coal car.

Boarding passengers, their train announced by the gateman, left the station, crossed the concourse, and descended the stairs. Tickets in hands, they found their coaches and Pullmans.

When everything was set, the conductor motioned for the flagman to remove his red light from the last car. With much hissing of steam and chugging of the huge pistons, the wheels began to turn. The fresh locomotive eased the train out of Union Station.

Probably the most famous of these passenger trains was the *Dixie Flyer* that ran between Chicago and Miami via Atlanta and enjoyed a good reputation for food and punctuality. It stayed twenty to twenty-five minutes beneath the shed while passengers got off and on, mail and baggage were handled, and locomotive number ninety-five, filled with fifteen thousand gallons of water and attached to its coal car, was put at the front. The *Dixie Flyer* had a fifteen-car limit with one engine; otherwise, it was "double-headed," or pulled by two engines. The staff of the famous dining car included three waiters, two cooks, and a dishwasher, whose cramped

quarters were adjacent to the kitchen in the car. In the smoking car, or lounge, a partition separated whites and blacks, although while in Tennessee no alcohol could be served legally to either race. Typically the *Dixie Flyer* included three Pullman sleepers. The crack train had a maximum speed of seventy-five miles per hour.

Of the special trains, the Barnum and Bailey Brothers circus trains seemed to lure more children, adults and railroad employees

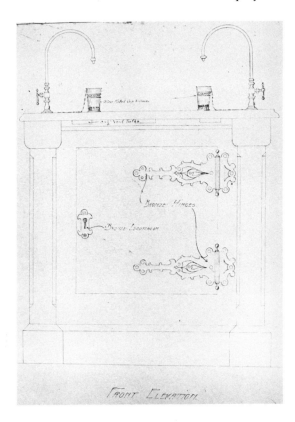

FRONT ELEVATION

Opposite Page: The Official Guide of the Railways *served as the bible of the railroad passenger business.*

Left: *Whites drank from one silver cup and Negroes from the other at the faucets in the main waiting room.*

65

to the Kayne Avenue yards than any other. As many as four trains and a total of one hundred cars brought the circus. The engineer and brakemen had to be careful not to jar the animals' cars because the sound and odor of steel chaffing in the couplings frightened the elephants. Freaks, the fat lady and the thin man, tattooed people, trapeze artists, and roustabouts unloaded from the passenger train. Animal cars had special hook-ups so they could be hauled straight out to Centennial Park where tents were erected and preparations begun for the circus. The following day the circus parade would return down Broad Street past the station while employees on the upper floors put their office windows to good use.

In 1924, two years after W.A. Anderton started handling mail, Van B. Wilson went to work inside Union Station in the traffic de-

*Two dozen long-distance passenger trains, several dozen freight trains, and numerous locals passed beneath the shed roof daily for more than fifty years.*

partment. The offices of the traffic department consisted of four large rooms on the second floor: the correspondence room, the rate room, the stenographers' pool, and the passenger traffic office. More than forty employees worked in the department. Interoffice communications went along the balcony overlooking the main waiting room. Access to each office was through one of the arches above which, in the spandrels, the ageless angels of Tennessee commerce held out their products.

Van B. Wilson's job was administrative, as opposed to Anderton's, which was operational. Wilson was a distribution clerk. Once the mail Anderton helped haul had been delivered to Union Station, it was sorted and marked in the correspondence room. Then Wilson distributed this marked mail to the appropriate offices. He also was responsible, along with another distribution clerk, for filing. The correspondence room had filing cabinets stacked floor to ceiling, with a rolling ladder providing access to the higher ones.

Wilson wore a suit and tie to work. He ate in the lunch room with other white collar employees. Once he had shown his ability as a distribution clerk, he was promoted to the rate room where he calculated freight tariffs.

Once Wilson figured a bill he leaned close to the funnel of a dictaphone and turned on the recording cylinder to verbalize the transaction. The cylinder was taken by a "runner" to the stenographers' pool where a transcriber (typist) listened to the cylinder and typed the bill. With hundreds of billings daily, the sound of typewriters clacking away in the stenographers' pool was a routine sound of the Union Station work day.

The rate room in which Wilson worked as a clerk was filled with desks, dictaphone funnels standing upright on most of them. The desks had been made in the railroad's own shops. Large sheets of glass covered their tops, with maps of every railroad line in the United States spread beneath the glass for easy rate-figuring reference. The big room was cooled by ceiling fans in the summer. Out the windows Wilson could see a fruit stand, a restaurant and the silhouettes of several small hotels where transient railroad personnel often boarded overnight. Terminal Lunch, "a little ole' pie wagon," was also below. A pie wagon was a retired trolley car with a diner-like atmosphere inside.

It was typical that the vicinity surrounding a large station contained a pie wagon, as well as hotels, boarding houses, newsstands, small eating places, and "joints," where a thirsty traveler or off-time railroad employee might find a drink.

The interior world of Union Station where Wilson worked and the outside world beneath the shed where Anderton worked were physically close together but otherwise far apart. Wilson and the administrative personnel were disconnected from the trains and the momentum of passenger traffic in a way that Anderton and those working beneath the shed and in the main waiting room were not.

The boss of everything that went on beneath the shed was the stationmaster. His superior, and the man responsible for every-thing inside the station as well as in all the yards, was the superintendent, whose office was on the third floor in the front, adjacent the tower. During the 1920s, J.P. Polk was superintendent. The offices of his staff, of the assistant superintendent, of the engineering and claims departments, and of the telegraph and relay people were also on the third floor, as were those of trainmasters and other per-sonnel of several railroad divisions.

By the 1920s many things had changed about Union Station. Major Lewis's alligators were a nostalgic memory. Large wooden doors painted with the letters *NC&St L* ob-scured the rectangular openings where the digital clock's canvas belts had failed to keep time. Two decades of constant smoke, both from the locomotives and the gulch, had mixed with rain and left tear-like stains down the limestone blocks and around the Roman-esque arches. Although not old, the station was taking on the patina of the Industrial Age.

Going downtown from the station in the early 1920s, many travelers still rode the trol-ley, but an ever increasing number of automo-biles used Broad Street as well. Going west on Broad toward the suburbs, one could still find livery stables, in addition to garages, coal yards, and other commercial businesses. About Sixteenth Avenue, residential neighbor-hoods began.

Union Station remained a center of atten-tion for entertainment despite the loss of Major Lewis's clock and alligators. Leisure time activities were still scarce in Nashville and parents often sent their children down to the station for an afternoon. Boys and girls sat on the stools of the soda fountain and fanta-sized about the travelers. The number of strangers, the excitement of trips, and the opulent surroundings of the barrel vault were still thrilling. Country people who only rarely came to the city continued to stare overhead as if in a daze. To them, to young people, and to even most adults, the station remained a fast-paced place promising romance and ex-citement. In an era when movie theatres were few and social life centered around the church, it was tantalizing to sit there sipping a Coke, thinking that a famous movie star might arrive or a politician—President Warren Harding and presidential contender Al Smith both visited during the 1920s—or at least a well-decorated soldier with a pretty girl on his arm.

The place still gave people a vicarious thrill. Teenagers felt very grown up being there. They overheard emotional goodbyes, saw funny incidents, and got a taste for the complex world in a way no other place in Nashville offered.

Both visitors and employees alike went outside the station the time the human spider climbed all over the limestone blocks, up past the rhythmic windows, beneath the gables, up the tower, past the boarded over clock, and touched (accounts vary about this) the winged heel of Mercury. A second exhibition, a dead whale, attracted and repelled people at the same time.

"The Health Department wouldn't let him get within fifty miles of the city now!" said Carl Cunningham, who saw the whale. "You could smell it all the way to Church Street. It was a big thing to go see the dead whale. I had never been to the ocean.

"My father and I went down to see the whale and we took every kid in the neighbor-hood in an A-Model Ford car. I think it cost twenty-five cents. They had lights strung up. It was a black mass. I guess it was a whale. It certainly stunk."

Not everyone loved Union Station, of course, and the environment it created had drawbacks. In the winter, on cold, windless days, a cloud could veil the gulch, the via-

*The stationmaster's office on the center staircase connecting the main concourse to the loading ramps.*

duct, and the yards. To suburbanites driving to work, the tower could be a grim spectre sticking out of a grey cloud. Even in fine weather the outside of the station usually had a grimy look. The experienced avoided walking across the viaduct in a white shirt or, if forced to, did not run a free hand along the rail; the fingers would come away black with soot. The railroad cleaned everything periodically, but each attempt seemed to leave the station a little darker than the previous cleaning had.

Well into the 1920s the restaurant in the northeast corner remained open, but competition from newer places soon closed its doors. Horse-cab drivers continued to compete for fares. Waiting around by the porte-cochère, they spent a fair amount of time speculating about the inevitable fall of Mercury—which way he might go, if someone would get hurt, where he would land. These anachronistic horsemen hung on to their profession despite the fact that almost everyone seemed to prefer to come and go to the station by automobile, even if they still drove a carriage at home. Hopelessly out of date, they calmed their animals when fenders came too close and horns blew too loudly. In a way they reminded one of the era that the railroads had just about brought to a close. The automobiles symbolized an era that was gathering great momentum. Union Station and the trains it served, at least for the time being, were in their middle years, aging symbols of progress between the animal transportation of the past and the family sedan of the future.

# Hard Times, Great Visitors

On the morning of November 11, 1934, ten thousand people surrounded Union Station. President Franklin D. Roosevelt was expected.

As the *Presidential Special* moved down the line, vigilant inspections of the tracks were carried out to detect possible sabotage. Soldiers guarded all the crossings. Hundreds of additional troops and policemen formed a ring of security around Union Station. Railroad carpenters made last minute inspections of the ramp they had built for the president's wheelchair. All about the station, on the viaduct, on Broad Street, in front of the brand-new post office, in the yards, elation, curiosity and confusion created an exciting aura. Never in the history of Nashville had there been so much anticipation, planning and worry over the four-hour visit of one man.

The sun was just lifting the fog when the *Presidential Special* pulled in. President Roosevelt rode up to street level in the baggage elevator, rolled down a special ramp aboard his wheelchair, and was loaded into a long black open-top touring car with his wife, Eleanor, and the governor of Tennessee, Hill McAlister. The president waved and smiled at the crowd.

After eating breakfast at the Maxwell House hotel, the Roosevelts and the governor went on a fifteen-mile motorcade parade through the streets of Nashville. They stopped at the Capitol, at Fisk University, and at several other places to make political speeches. President Roosevelt was promoting his New Deal, which had funded construction of the post office adjacent to Union Station and which was attempting to lift America out of the Great Depression. Well over one hundred thousand men, women and children thronged the route; it was the largest public gathering in the history of Nashville.

President Roosevelt returned again in 1936, but for a more solemn occasion. Tennessee Congressman Joseph W. Byrns, who was Speaker of the House and a Roosevelt supporter, had died. As the train bringing President Roosevelt and the coffin towards Nashville passed through town after town, all the churches tolled their bells. Again, railroad inspectors checked the tracks and soldiers stood on guard at every crossing.

The contrasting elation and gloom of the two presidential trips to Nashville were symbolic of the contradictory nature of the depression decade. Famous visitors and parades stood out in sharp contrast to widespread unemployment, bread lines, and poverty. It was the worst of times, yet occasionally certain people and events made it seem the best of times. Optimism flowered even in the general despair.

During these years Union Station employees fared better than most people. Despite reduced revenues and traffic, the railroads still ran. They remained the commercial lifeblood of a sick economy. Both the L&N and the NC&St L reduced working hours so that everyone stayed on the payroll. Few new people were hired. Reduction in the work force came about through attrition. Old seniority lists show gaps of three and four years during which not one clerk or ticket seller or mail handler was hired.

*Sidewalk superintendents watch progress on the post office during the depression.*

Railroad families looked to their fellow railroad families for comfort, support and recreation even more than they had before. Long-time Nashville Mayor Richard Fulton, whose father was a signal foreman for forty-seven years, remembered families getting together once a month just to get together. For fun his mother would take him and the other three children on weekend train rides with free passes. They traveled to Louisville or St. Louis or some other city within a day's train ride, switched coaches, then returned to Nashville. To the mayor's youthful eyes Union Station was a castle and the trips were a joy. As for other memories, he said with a smile, "I got a nose full of cinders on those trips."

Things almost taken for granted in the 1920s gained renewed appreciation: the sound

*President Roosevelt, his wife Eleanor, and, at the left, Governor Hill McAllister went on a motorcade through the streets of Nashville.*

of a band playing on the concourse, the sight of an ecstatic wedding party, the glimpse of a white gown disappearing into a Pullman sleeper. An extraordinary number of couples got married during the decade; rice thrown by well-wishers always seemed to be on the concourse stairs.

College students continued to add a cheerful, rowdy air to the station when they left for school or came home from vacations. Young enough to ignore the dismal job prospects facing them upon graduation, the students yelled down the length of the shed, laughed loudly, and carried their tennis rackets and bird cages into the passenger cars.

Football had become a popular spectator sport and large numbers of fans, as well as visiting teams, arrived aboard trains for Vanderbilt games. One of the more unusual of these steamed into Nashville several weeks after President Roosevelt's visit. In October, 1934, Senator Huey Long of Louisiana commandeered enough coaches and locomotives to bring seven thousand loyal fans north to cheer on LSU in a game against the Vanderbilt Commodores. The notorious Kingfish, blending cant, rabble-rousing, and bayou wisdom, was making a bid for the presidential nomination. *Tennessean* reporter John Thompson witnessed the visit and described the red carpet treatment rolled out for Huey Long.

"The whole staff of *The Tennessean* evening and morning just turned to and hung to his every word and got as near to him as we could in the parade and took pictures of him. And it was all together something. I've never seen such—the Second Coming of Christ couldn't have had such coverage."

A total of twenty thousand spectators came to Dudley Field to see the game and to get a glimpse of the Kingfish, and he did not let them down. He joined the cheerleaders on occasion, led the parade at half time, delivered a speech, and apparently inspired the

*A 1938 Vanderbilt University pep rally takes place at Union Station as the football team leaves for a game.*

LSU players who trounced Vanderbilt by a score of twenty-nine to nothing. Before leading his all-Negro band, his team, and the seven thousand fans back aboard the trains at Union Station, Long told the press that after LSU his most favorite football team was Vanderbilt. He had wanted to win, but such a lopsided victory verged on humiliation.

One final visitor of note during the 1930s stayed only a few minutes beneath the shed of Union Station. Chicago mobster Al Capone passed through on his way to a penitentiary in Atlanta aboard the *Dixie Flyer*. He rode in a private coach with bars on the windows and guards at the doors. Undaunted and sympathetic, Western Union messenger W.W. Pinkleton managed to get close to the gangster's window.

*"The Kingfish," Senator Huey Long of Louisiana, parades arm-in-arm through Nashville with Mayor Hilary Howse.*

*Eleanor Roosevelt disembarks from the Presidential Special in 1936.*

"He was handcuffed," Pinkleton remembered. "His right arm was handcuffed to the arm rest and he was handcuffed to an FBI agent with his left arm. The car was quite loaded with FBI agents. I talked with the porter on the train, and he was very happy because Mr. Capone had given him a ten dollar tip which would be about a hundred dollars today.

"Income tax evasion, I believe, was what they sentenced him for. . . . As I went back upstairs, I know I worried about it. . . . I really worried about the fact that the man had eleven years to spend [in prison], even though he was responsible for a lot of crimes."

# World War II

If Union Station had a greatest period, the World War II years were it. The station was the center of a complex web of bases, training facilities, supply depots, and prisoner-of-war camps located around the city and throughout Middle Tennessee. The state proved an ideal place for so many military installations because it was centrally located, sparsely populated, and topographically similar to the embattled landscape of much of Eastern Europe. At any one time three to five hundred thousand men were training, traveling, or participating in war games and maneuvers in Middle Tennessee. Almost all of these men, at one time or another, laid eyes on the "man running to catch a train."

Beginning in December, 1941, departures of volunteers charged the station in a way only war can electrify the atmosphere. Many times the main waiting room, the concourse, and the ramps between the trains were so crammed with families, lovers and friends sending men off to fight that redcaps and mail handlers could hardly get through. Using megaphones, the gatemen seemed to be announcing trains constantly. Long lines of soldiers and civilians serpentined across the main waiting room floor, everyone shuffling toward the nine ticket windows. Goodbyes were tense and draining. Young men, often for the first time, saw their fathers break into tears. Embraces lasted for minutes. Where rice had sprinkled the concourse stairs during the depression, now tears dampened them. Trains departed and mothers held children aloft, their puzzled lips giving Daddy a last kiss goodbye. Moved, some of the men smiled; others wore glazed looks. Once the train disappeared from sight, heads hung. Voices were quiet. Red Cross volunteers returned to their canteen hut and solemn well-wishers made their way back up the stairs and out to their cars.

The combined work force of the NC&St L and the L&N in Nashville during the height of the war numbered nearly three thousand people. That did not include the hundreds of volunteer hostesses and Red Cross workers who staffed their facilities around the clock.

For both railroad help and volunteers, working at the station was arduous yet filled with dutiful purpose. The railroads were the lifeline of the huge, complex network of men, materiel and arms that would bring about

77

Below: *A mother holds her daughter aloft to kiss Daddy goodbye.*

Opposite page: *Volunteers depart for military duty.*

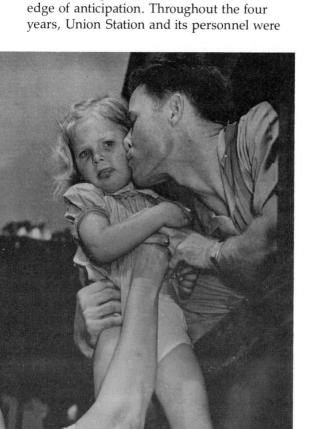

victory. A grim optimism infused even the toughest days. All three shifts might be busy or, if no troop trains arrived, calm but with an edge of anticipation. Throughout the four years, Union Station and its personnel were taxed and strained in ways they never had been before.

Part of the solution to this overtaxing was a resource the L&N and the NC&St L had long ignored: women. They might not make good engineers or switchmen, but for other positions the old policy of "men only" had to change.

Mary Loftin (who would eventually marry traffic agent Van B. Wilson who worked on the second floor) had just graduated from college when the war broke out. Her father worked as a ticket clerk at the station, so she had grown up with railroad lingo and understood the *Railroad Guide*, the bible of the business. One afternoon in early 1942 she was down at the station picking up her father, and a few afternoons later she was cubbing as a ticket clerk. After three weeks she got a cash box, a ticket window, a ticket die with her number on it for stamping tickets, and was added to the payroll.

From her window in the row of nine, Loftin sold tickets as quickly and as efficiently as possible. Over the purchasers' shoulders she caught glimpses of families and friends sending their loved ones off to war, of raw recruits wandering around seeking directions, of men in uniform glancing up at the Tennessee angels of commerce and at the stained-glass ceiling. Many had a faraway look in their eyes.

Selling tickets all day was a responsible job for a young woman. It required alertness and discretion. Loftin had to decide if a passenger could use a check. She kept her own

cash box. Bad checks and cash shortages were
both deducted from her pay. Standing on her
feet for hours on end, sometimes eating lunch
while stamping tickets and counting money,
Loftin asked what seemed an endless succes-
sion of young strangers where they wanted to
go. Sometimes there was so much money
changing hands she could hardly keep up
with it.

In the main waiting room everything was
usually busy during the day: the lunch room,
the newsstand with headlines about the Pa-
cific and the European fronts, the Western
Union office, the parcel check, and the soda
fountain across from the ticket windows. In
the evening things calmed down, although
the arrival of a troop train late at night
brought the hostesses to their feet and
charged the air with the energy of young soldiers, most of them lonely, wanting someone
to talk to.

The railroad continued to hire women
ticket clerks and they soon numbered thirty-
two, three-fourths of the staff. They became
an integral part of the efficient machine that
was Union Station.

In effect, the station handled warfare
needs and traffic, with leftover room in the
coaches allotted to nonmilitary passengers.
Civilians lucky enough to get tickets often had
to sit on their luggage in the aisles while ex-
hausted troops slept in the seats. As during
World War I, most passenger coaches were
put to military use. Boxcars, their sides cut
open as windows, benches bolted to their
floors, also transported soldiers. More than a

hundred trains a day passed through the station. Some double-headed trains carried several thousand troops at a time, their destinations secret. Volunteers from the Red Cross canteen walked beneath the windows of the parked troop trains, offering the boys coffee and doughnuts, postcards, smiles, bits of conversation, and, hundreds of times, their addresses. The canteen was only one of several USO (United Service Organization) and Red Cross services in the station.

As soon as war had been declared in December, 1941, the canteen, a fixture during World War I, had been reactivated. Hastily tying Red Cross arm bands around their heads, volunteers set up a table in the main waiting room and got the railroad to clean out a hut by the tracks. The USO, which was a combined effort of the YMCA, YWCA, Salvation Army, Travelers' Aid, and other groups, opened a lounge in the northeast room where the restaurant had been and began serving meals four days after Pearl Harbor. Staffed twenty-four hours a day, this room was usually either mobbed with uniformed men or practically empty; soldiers did not arrive at Union Station a few at a time. Occasionally a pianist entertained or a dance offered the soldiers a better chance to socialize.

During the first year of the war nearly a

*Prior to the war, railroad hiring policy excluded women. A shortage of able-bodied men changed that. First row, left to right: Era Strane Davis, Ruby Ray, Sarah Warren, Roberta Shumate (Heflin), Watina Reeves (Schoenberger), Mary Harding Loftin (Wilson), Jane Vassar, Betty Hicks, Alma Whitaker, Mrs. Thanial Finley, Roberta Schlosser, H.W. Loftin, and W.A Lightfoot. Second row, from left: Mamie Sanders, Nancy Waddell (Grubbs), Vivian Whitehead (Brame), Carrie J. Fitzgerald (Coats), Mary Gilbert King (Mathis), Etta Davis, Lorraine McGowan, Nell Alex, Jane Joslin (Terry), and Ellen Moran (Pinson). Third row, from left: Alice Davant, Christine Harbison, Jane Schweitzer (Smith), Dorothy Davis (Bass), Flossie Keaton, Elynor Rooney, Mabel Ogilvie, Marianna Schlosser.*

million soldiers passed through Nashville. To demonstrate the city's support of the troops, the USO established a network of hospitality accommodations in college dormitories, church basements, private houses, and anywhere else there was a spare bed. Shortages of beds still occurred and on many mornings hundreds of soldiers could be found sleeping in the parks, on the floor of Union Station, on the steps of the post office next door, or in the arms of prostitutes in the red-light district below Capitol Hill. Not all the soldiers cared for the kinds of comfort the USO provided and the red-light district was an area with hundreds of prostitutes, dozens of card games, and free-flowing alcohol only a twenty-minute walk from Union Station.

Every facility in Nashville was taxed to its limits by the war. The population of the city ballooned and deflated and ballooned again. Men in uniform came by train from all the nearby camps and training areas. Camp Forrest, seventy miles south in Tullahoma, typically had seventy thousand soldiers. The Army Air Corps at Berry Field had ten thousand. On Thompson Lane where One Hundred Oaks shopping mall sits today, another ten thousand men were at any one time being screened for pilot, navigator, bombadier, and other flight-related assignments for the entire Air Corps. The Second Army conducted maneuvers, war games, and various exercises all over the countryside. At Fort Campbell on the Kentucky border were stationed another fifty thousand men. One sequence of training ma-

neuvers in 1943 and 1944 brought approximately six hundred thousand soldiers and airmen to the state.

It was after a series of these maneuvers when an avalanche of men in uniform hit Union Station. Tens of thousands of soldiers came streaming in, looking for something to do. Neither Nashville nor Union Station could handle them. A worried superintendent J.P. Polk called Jeannette Acklen Noel, who worked for the Red Cross, and said, "We're in serious condition down here."

Soldiers were everywhere; they swarmed over the concourse, the waiting rooms, the balcony. The shelves of the lunch room were bare and the booths filled. More soldiers were arriving even as those already there napped in every available corner. Jeannette Noel did not let the numbers overwhelm her.

"There was this little store called the Little Market Basket on Granny White Pike," she said, "and I just went in there—I knew the manager—and I told him I didn't have any money or tickets and the two heads of the Red Cross were out of the city, but . . . this is an emergency. I bought every piece of cold meat he had, one hundred loaves of bread, and three cases of eggs. I called up the Ramsey pie people and told them to send me two thousand pies. Well, when I got to Union Station the phone was ringing, and this man wanted to speak to Mrs. Noel. . . . He said, 'Well, Mrs. Noel, we just wanted to tell you what happened. A darn fool woman called up here and ordered two thousand pies in your

*Three seasoned travelers wait patiently on stacked grain bags and a suitcase.*

name.' I said, 'Oh no she didn't, I did, and you better get them down here in a hurry—this is an emergency!

"He said, 'We haven't got them.'

"I said, 'Start cooking.'

"They sent me about five hundred pies first. That was all they had. I said that I didn't care if they were a day old, send them on down here."

That day the Red Cross canteen served five thousand meals.

By 1943, such feats, if not common, were numerous enough to be taken in stride. The war had created carnage, death, and heroics in such vast proportions that they were almost a matter of course. By this time everyone in Nashville knew families whose sons had died in combat, or had known the boys themselves. Goodbyes accompanied by assurances of a quick triumph became rare. The costs in human life had made them sound hollow. Sad farewells were more common, filled with irresolvable tension and discernible fear.

"The most pathetic part of the whole lot of it was to see mothers, wives and children there to see their husbands off," V.T. Nelms, who worked in the stationmaster's office, said. "We all knew that some of them would never come back. And these things were heartrending. . . . When they would go out, we couldn't help sometimes having tears in our eyes."

Handling the departures of many of these troops and shouldering the responsibility for everything that happened beneath the shed roof on third trick (11:00 P.M. until 7:00 A.M.) was W.A. Anderton. The farmer from Bell Buckle who had thought Union Station was a mighty big place in 1922 had become a stationmaster.

Describing the difficulty of his job during the war, Anderton said, "It was rough."

Double-headed troop trains pulled so many cars that they extended both north and

*Goodbyes filled with emotion were the norm.*

south of the shed, blocking everything. It was an unending challenge to get these troop trains in and out on time.

Getting good help was another problem. The attrition policy of the depression years had created a shortage of trained yard men. Enlistments had made things worse. There was a constant shortage of decent maintenance and operations personnel. Added to that was the fact that equipment relegated to the scrap heap had been brought back into service. In the new shops old men brought back to work repaired junked locomotives and cars.

One young man who became an engineer during these years was J.J. Kinnard. Kinnard had been one of the first firemen hired after the Depression. The man above him on the seniority list was sixty. Kinnard was twenty-five.

As the youngest fireman he had plenty of opportunity to hand fire the locomotives; the stokers went with the older firemen. Dangers on the job centered around running out of water. The engine could blow up. If you thought that was about to happen, "You were off that engine like a flying squirrel," Kinnard recalled.

During the war promotions came fast. Once he was an engineer, Kinnard realized he had never really gotten the feeling of running a locomotive while firing. You had to be on the other side, he claimed, on the engineer's side. But then, "You actually felt that train in the seat of your britches. There was a real art to running a steam locomotive."

During the war Kinnard often ran double headers pulling sixty-five to seventy cars of gasoline. He hauled tanks and airplane wings on flat cars, soldiers in coaches and boxcars, prisoners-of-war in barred cars, and soft coal in coal cars, stockpiling it along the tracks. Huge stockpiles were maintained at certain intervals, insuring adequate fuel in case of an attack.

President Roosevelt made a third stop at

*Embraces lasted for minutes.*

*Two businessmen bid women goodbye.*

Union Station during the war, but this time his stay was even briefer than his visits in the 1930s had been. His presence was kept a secret; he just passed through.

When the war ended in 1945, jubilant engineers blew their steam whistles. Mail handlers kissed canteen workers. Redcaps threw their hats up above the cones of light. People felt as if a tremendous weight had been lifted. They went wild. There was dancing and drinking and hugging. Crowds surged out the front of Union Station through the arches and joined the crowds on Broad Street. People paraded through the city and back and forth into the station all night long as whistles blew, bells rang, and tears flowed. The boys were coming home.

# From Pullmans to Pontiacs

Postwar Nashville boomed, but a significant change occurred. Union Station, so busy during the war, was no longer the hub of things. Suddenly a new breed of businessman and politician, many of whom were returning veterans, wanted exactly what Major Lewis and his supporters had wanted for Nashville in the 1890s: *the force*. Except now instead of the railroad and a big station *the force* was cars and highways, with airplanes whirling their props in the wings.

Esteem for Union Station plummeted, as if wartime heroics had used it up. For people who wanted to be modern, and that included most, the family sedan was "in," not a ride on the *Hummingbird*, even if it was the "train of the future." To some the term "train of the future" seemed little more than a humorous contradiction; the words *train* and *future* did not belong in the same sentence.

In Nashville the Chamber of Commerce promoted traffic improvements, like widening streets and extending new ones out into the growing suburbs. Boys and girls talked about traveling in Pontiacs, not Pullmans. Slowly but noticeably the number of travelers using Union Station decreased. For every personal-

ity arriving by train—Dizzy Dean the baseball great passed through regularly; Mae West, who entertained at Ryman Auditorium, got stranded here during the "Blizzard of '51"—another one drove or tried hopping from airport to airport until he or she glided down onto Nashville's Berry Field. Union Station remained a way to arrive in the city, but it was only one of several ways.

Statistics tell the tale. Between 1945 and 1950 the L&N's passenger traffic (including the NC&St L) dropped seventy-five percent, from ten million passengers to about two and one-half million. By 1958, rail travelers on the L&N barely exceeded one million for the year. Over a thirteen-year period, therefore, passenger business declined ninety percent at a time when Americans were traveling more than they ever had.

At first the railroads attempted to compete by designing trains like the *Hummingbird*, which had aluminum passenger cars with glass-dome roofs. Advertising was stepped up. But the love affair between the American and his car already had a momentum that surpassed anything railroad management could derail. To the young, in particular, the

train was old-fashioned, something their grandparents rode.

In 1949, when passenger business was declining rapidly but still viable, the L&N upgraded Union Station as part of a modernization campaign. Escalators were installed and fresh paint brightened the coffers and medallions of the main waiting room. A roof was built over the main concourse to protect travelers from the weather.

Ironically, as travelers chose alternatives to trains, the smoke that had made rail travel so dirty disappeared because diesel engines replaced steam locomotives. The cinder showers of old were no more, but families didn't care; trains now meant waiting at blinking red lights while Granddad, if he was along on the trip, reminisced about the L&N.

In Union Station four ticket windows were more than enough to handle customers. Then, in 1952, Mercury fell from the tower. It was a bad omen. That same year the powerful truck lobby made inroads on a long-time rail monopoly, the mail.

Business continued to decrease until 1957 when the L&N vacated the upper floors of Union Station and consolidated its offices in Louisville. The ticket office staff, from a war-time high of more than forty agents, now numbered six. They sold approximately three hundred tickets a day for the twenty-one passenger trains still passing through, or about fifteen per train. The NC&St L ceased to exist as a subsidiary and its personnel moved to Radnor yards where most of the freight was handled. The white oak treads of the interior

Opposite page: *Union Station after World War II when the family sedan was fast becoming the way to travel.*

This page: *A modernization program in 1949 brought this shiny new escalator to Union Station and put a fresh coat of paint on the ceiling of the main waiting room.*

stairways gathered dust, as did their never-used replacements in the attic. The upper floors of Union Station were empty and quiet.

Arriving at the station then, a passenger might have had difficulty finding a redcap. Gatemen in worn uniforms still called trains but most of the time they pushed brooms instead.

All the local accommodations had ceased operation years before. It was emblematic of the crossover between reality and nostalgia that when the Lebanon accommodation had been canceled, a large number of citizens appeared at the public hearing to protest the end of their local service. The railroad spokesman asked the most vocal protester how he had come to Nashville that morning.

"By automobile," the man replied

Asked the same question, ninety percent of the others said they had driven.

*Young passengers bound for Mammoth Cave in 1953.*

"Well?" the spokesman asked.

The protest died.

The one corner of the station that increased its business during those years was the lunch room. By offering 1960s-style fast food it was ahead of its time. At noon four waitresses served sandwiches, hot plates, and pie to employees of the post office, the Customs House, and even to some travelers. After a quick lunch a man could still get a good haircut and a shoe shine.

During the 1960s hold-out passengers consisted of rail buffs, old people who had not adapted, a few long-haired college students with backpacks, and those who were afraid to fly. Often they packed their own lunches because the dining car, that restaurant on wheels, had become in most instances a parody of its former self. The break-even point in a dining car operation was two hundred and twenty-five percent of capacity, meaning the car had to feed more than twice the number of people it could seat at maximum efficiency merely to break even. And

*Traffic on Broad increased as railroad traffic declined.*

"maximum efficiency" was a joke when slow, shuffling waiters brought out bad food and the windows rattled as customers ate it. Pullman cars needed to run at one hundred and twenty-five percent. It was no wonder that both dining and sleeping cars were disappearing from the remaining lines.

This loss of elegance, of that special graciousness of train travel, was the *coup de grâce* for many hold outs. They balked at mere utility over poorly maintained tracks and at the need often to lug their luggage out through a deserted depot only to find that the cabs were all at the airport. In such a situation it was hard not to want to join the thousands who arrived and departed Nashville every day by air—Union Station was an anachronism and if you used it so were you.

It got so bad that by the 1970s two ticket windows sold an average of one hundred tickets daily. Then Amtrak took over and the ticket office moved to the baggage building.

In 1974 Union Station looked grim. The entrance arches were boarded up, the limestone looked filthy, and pigeons perched on the roof and flew in and out of openings, suggesting the station was now a rookery. Ticket sales continued from the baggage building and a corner of the ladies' waiting room had been sectioned off as a waiting area for the few passengers. Standing there, they could look down through dirty glass at the railroad tracks and hear the cooing pigeons overhead.

# Pigeons and Politicians

## 11

Today, it is in peril from the wreckers, an island in the midst of automobile traffic hurrying to the airports which helped seal its doom.
—Thomas B. Brumbach, *Architecture of Middle Tennessee*

Even as a ruin Union Station remained formidable. All that bulk and history standing empty and sad was enough to make passersby familiar with the station's past avert their eyes, as though encountering a man in tatters and low spirits who had once commanded Nashville's respect. Union Station had become the bag person of downtown architecture.

In January, 1975, reporter Louise Davis decided to take a look at the limestone derelict. Amtrak personnel from the baggage building let her in. The air was cold and dank. Shades had been pulled down over the ticket windows. The passenger benches were shoved against the walls, making room for a huge puddle. Overhead the stained glass looked dirty, the angels of Tennessee commerce forlorn. Davis was told a story about a railroad man coming in to check out his old haunt. The place had so depressed him he thought he was dead.

"There is not a gloomier spot in Nashville," she wrote in *The Tennessean Magazine* on February 2, 1975.

But her article also recounted the grandeur of the station's past and its importance in Tennessee history. She described Mayor Head's opening day speech that had sealed the Tennessee Central's doom, told how the first locomotive arrived in Nashville on a barge, explained how the accommodations had operated, evoked the emotion that had made the tears of war flow, and established in every reader's mind that this rundown Goliath of Nashville architecture was not so much a dingy landmark but rather a symbol of the city's spirit and soul. If Nashville had to be distilled into one building, the article implied, Union Station was it.

An unprecedented response followed. One reader volunteered to scrub the grimy outside clean, if that was needed. Others told of peering down at Major Lewis's alligators in the pools. Some recalled Mercury on the roof or the day he tumbled. Still others remembered the digital clock, eating in the elegant restaurant in the 1920s, crying as loved ones left for war, hurrying to the tracks to watch elephants and tigers from the circus unload.

One reader was so moved that she confessed, "I cried when I read the story."

At that time much of Nashville's historic architecture seemed to be awaiting the wrecker's ball. Suburban living, shopping malls, and free parking epitomized the 1970s, not blackened limestone monuments, dank interiors, and vacant lots downtown. Preservation momentum was gathering, however, as more and more people hated to see their city's past gutted with indifference and often replaced with buildings lacking character or out of harmony with their surroundings. The public concern shown for Union Station in the wake of Louise Davis's article identified a single structure preservationists could focus on.

Fletch Coke was one of these preservationists. "There was not one shining light downtown in historic preservation," she said of those days. The Hermitage Hotel was locked up. The Custom House had been declared surplus property. An insurance company owned Ryman Auditorium, which had lost the Grand Ole Opry, and wanted to strip the interior and use it to build a little chapel out at Opryland. If there was a glimmer of promise it came from the repainted fronts of several warehouses along Second Avenue. Union Station's emergence as a truly loved place brought much needed hope that more preservation work would follow. Yet the overriding question remained: what could be done with a soot-covered relic in a declining downtown?

Union Station needed a sympathetic investor, and efforts were made to find one.

These included Historic Nashville's SOS, or "Save Our Station" workshop, which brought together speakers, politicians and preservationists to discuss what might be done. In attendance were New York architect Norman Pfeiffer who had written *Reusing Railroad Stations* and Fred Hutton who had built a scale model of Union Station. Something seemed to want to happen, but nobody knew quite what. The derelict station was just too big, formidable and daunting for a group of volunteers to attack on weekends. Any great change in a great building was going to need plenty of cash and vision. No one with either came rushing forward.

To educate the public about the station's past and to keep hope alive for its future, the Junior League funded *Speaking of Union Station*, an oral history. Four interviewers taped the memories of more than one hundred people who had worked at or used the station, including some who had witnessed its construction and others who had been among the nervous young ladies from Ward's Seminary who had dropped Tennessee products into an urn on October 9, 1900. A "Whistle Stop Tea Dance" kicked off the book's publication. Several hundred people, many in period costumes, showed up to dance, reminisce and buy books on the main concourse.

That same year, 1977, brought designated National Historic Landmark status to the station and shed. Shortly thereafter, in an apparent stroke of good luck, the federal government came to the station's rescue.

The General Services Administration

*An angel in need of care.*

*Fletch Coke, with her daughter Alice and Senator Jim Sasser looking on, testifies at a hearing before the U.S. Senate Committee on Public Works.*

(GSA) under President Carter had decided to help revitalize downtowns by funding preservation projects. Jay Solomon, head administrator of the GSA, was from Chattanooga. He declared that Union Station was going to become a precedent; it would lead the way in the restoration of derelict architectural gems in America's urban cores.

The railroad cooperated and sold the station to the GSA for one dollar. A flurry of plans and announcements followed. Soon it was being said that $8 million would be spent converting dingy Union Station into federal and state offices. The Romanesque white elephant was saved, the papers claimed, and the

Senate was "flashing the green light and clearing the track." The GSA, which in fact had little experience in preservation, was praised for its preservation expertise. Fletch Coke traveled to Washington and testified before the Senate Committee on Public Works. She pinched herself to make sure she wasn't dreaming. After the committee approved the money for Union Station, Senator Patrick Moynihan said, "This is really a bargain for the government."

Tennessee politicians tripped over each other in a rush to agree. It was said that by 1980 the main waiting room would be restored to its original splendor and new offices would fill the building.

An immediate hurdle to the plans were the pigeons that had turned Union Station into their rookery. Michael Emrick, an architect who had worked on the Historic Structure Report for the government, provided the authorities with a "pigeon-droppings contour map." It was an important document. The threat of histoplasmosis, the pigeon-droppings disease, had to be eradicated before any architect, workman or bureaucrat could safety enter the station.

Experts gassed the station. But the experts were not experts on pigeon behavior. The birds found ways out, waited for the gas to disperse, and then flew back in.

Meanwhile, other things started going wrong. The railroad had hardly transferred ownership of the station to the GSA in September, 1978, when Jay Solomon found himself in some hot water. Mud slinging began. A

94

report claimed that Solomon was serving his own interests, that Union Station was his pet project, and that the GSA had misled Congress. Senator Jim Sasser came to Solomon's defense, but despite his contentions that Solomon was only exposing fraud in the GSA (his accusations eventually resulted in forty-one indictments and twenty-seven guilty pleas for defrauding the government), the administrator soon resigned his post and Union Station, as dirty and forlorn as ever, became identified with him. The project seemed in jeopardy.

Work did not visibly slow down, though, because it had never visibly begun. Then a company from the Bronx, New York, erected scaffolding around the entire station so it could be made weathertight for the fumigators, and things seemed about to happen.

Despite space suited workmen appearing on the scaffolding suddenly, the pigeons did not want to vacate. Maligned in the press, grumbled about in the streets, and slandered by the health department, the pigeons hung in there. Health officials continued to insist that the birds and their droppings must be cleaned out of Union Station before architects, engineers or workmen entered. The scaffolding, a reminder to every passing motorist of how ridiculous this whole situation was becoming, merely provided additional perches for more birds. As time dragged on the scaffolding became the brunt of jokes.

"What Goes Up at $474,000 Just Won't Come Down, Yet," one headline read. The GSA defended the scaffolding, claiming it might be needed soon. A spokesman for the scaffolding company in New York admitted he didn't know what was going on. He kept abreast of the pigeon wars by telephoning a receptionist at the Sheraton across the street, he said. She peeked outside and reported back if it looked as though anything was happening.

Little was.

*Dressed in protective clothing fumigators neutralize pigeon droppings to prevent histoplasmosis.*

Above: *Pigeons turned Union Station into a rookery.*

Opposite page: *"What Goes Up at $474,000 Just Won't Come Down, Yet," a newspaper headline said about the scaffolding.*

In October, 1979, after more than one hundred and twenty-five years of service, Nashville heard the last whistle from a regular passenger train. The *Floridian*, which seldom ran on time and when it did seemed either to bake or freeze passengers, left Union Station with twenty-two history-makers on board. Once it disappeared the pigeons had the damp building all to themselves.

Fumigators again tried and again failed to rid the station of the pigeons and their toxic droppings, and accusations started flying: the GSA was wasting time and money; this job was never going to start. Even some politicians admitted the project was not going smoothly.

It seemed a classic case of bureaucratic bungling: two years, $1 million, nothing changed. An editorial in the Nashville *Tennessean* on August 5, 1980, summed up the stalemate: "The war between the pigeons and the General Services Administration for control of Nashville's 80-year-old Union Station is continuing, with the pigeons getting the upper hand. . . . The secret is that the pigeons want to win the war."

Senator Sasser announced that he would ask the GSA to file weekly reports on progress at Union Station. The regional administrator of the GSA insisted that his agency was fighting the pigeons every day. He threw the feathers back into the senator's lap when he added that the real problem was the whole Nashville area; it was a "haven for the birds."

This sounded like a scare tactic.

Through the rest of 1980 the pigeons remained and the paper shuffling continued. Finally, loud demands for any kind of action whatsoever from the GSA prompted the agency to revise its strategy. There was a $1.8 million cost overrun on this project, it was announced. That was how much money had been spent to eliminate the pigeons that were still there. In a move that reinforced the gathering suspicion that the real pigeons were the citizens of Nashville, the GSA said the cost overrun meant the Union Station project had to be reduced in scope.

In March, 1981, work was again slated to begin on the reduced plan when an "oversight" was discovered. Someone had forgotten to budget the $350 thousand needed to pay the architects and engineers to design new plans. Work would have to be postponed until fall, presuming there would be funds available then.

The fiasco had drifted into the absurd. From a feeling of good fortune smiling down on the grimy station in 1977, the feeling now was that a political vendetta riddled with pre-*1984* double-speak was in progress. Jay Solomon had stepped on some important toes and they were kicking the Union Station project to death.

Finally, in July, the GSA admitted that the project "has been snake bit" from the start.

The implication suddenly motivated everybody. In October the fumigators finally

96

ousted the pigeons. Architects and engineers entered the station for structural tests and design review. The scaffolding, after becoming a kind of Nashville landmark in its own right, was dismantled and disappeared, taking the pressure off the receptionist at the Sheraton.

In January, 1982, in yet another revision downwards, the GSA approved a $4.75 million plan to create thirty-eight thousand square feet of office space in Union Station. Summer arrived but no work began. Behind the scenes the whole thing was starting to unravel. Mayor Richard Fulton came out publicly in favor of having private developers step in to rescue the station. Reports began circulating that office space needs in Nashville had been eliminated by other construction and that Union Station was for sale.

The story had come full circle. Nashville, so eager to save Union Station in 1977, had turned to the GSA and now was faced with the task of getting the building free from the clutches of the bumbling savior. Historic Nashville was disgusted with the whole affair. It threatened to sue the GSA for failure to meet the original 1977 contract.

By this time downtown Nashville was on the upswing. Second Avenue had become a point of pride, several blocks of attractive Italianate warehouses having been turned into restaurants, stores, offices and apartments. Other abandoned buildings were gaining attention. Private development of Union Station now seemed possible whereas a few years ago it had been a dream. Mayor Fulton wanted some seed money with which to attract pro-

spective developers to the huge station project, but the GSA only offered to pay for more studies.

There was no more need for studies. Union Station had been studied to death.

In February, 1983, Senator William Proxmire presented the whole boondoggle his Golden Fleece award, which was given for lavish wastes of taxpayers' dollars. Proxmire said the station deserved the award because there had been "far too many boo boos made while trying to renovate this old choo-choo station." Stop making a pigeon out of the taxpayer, Proxmire urged.

Historic Nashville filed suit to force compliance by the GSA to the 1977 contract. The suit demanded the funds remaining from the original $7.1 million that had been allocated. The GSA showed signs of cooperating, then tried to wiggle free by offering Nashville a quick $105,000 thousand.

"One hundred and five thousand dollars wouldn't pay to sweep the pigeon droppings out of there," Mayor Fulton responded.

At least the potential was there for someone to take the risk no one would consider taking five years before. From ten years before when a handful of people had not wanted to see Union Station razed, now a great many people wanted old buildings saved and developers were more willing to invest in their futures. The revived enthusiasm for tomorrow seemed reminiscent of the days of Major Lewis and the construction of Union Station, except in the mid-1980s historical architecture had become part of this future, not something to be knocked down and discarded.

Mayor Fulton appointed a committee to review proposals from developers interested in Union Station. In September, 1983, the announcement was made that Elkington and Keltner Development of Memphis, developers involved in Beal Street, would lease the station, buy the shed from the railroad, and turn the property into a complex of restaurants, shops, offices, and a hotel. A local company, CRC Equities, soon became a partner.

More tedious dealings between the city and the GSA resulted in ownership of Union Station passing back to Nashville. The federal agency allocated $1.5 million for stabilization of the structure, and Historic Nashville dropped its suit.

*Mayor Richard Fulton shows developers the deteriorated* Bully 108.

# A Ruin Transformed

In the late summer of 1985, Leon Moore and Richard Johnson were driving around Nashville, looking for a possible site to build a "suite" concept hotel. As they passed Union Station, on which restoration work had yet to begin, Johnson said jokingly, "Why don't we put one in there?"

Moore and Johnson were developers with ambitions. Their company, Gulf Coast Development, Inc., built, owned, and operated a number of Shoney's inns, including one in Nashville. Neither man was adverse to risk. They knew that Elkington and Keltner had not followed through on its initial plans and that the purchase of the shed, which the railroad still owned, was up in the air.

Johnson called Congressman Bill Boner's office and he and Moore toured the station. Except for the lack of pigeons, it had not changed much since Louise Davis had walked in almost ten years before. Vandals had wrestled the wooden crowns off newel posts and leaks had weakened floor joists and bulged plaster, but the aura of authenticity and sense of potential were still there. Moore and Johnson realized they could do something

with it; they had the skills, employees and desire to both rehabilitate Union Station and then manage it as a hotel. After meeting with Elkington and Keltner and CRC Equities, the original developers, they took the lagging project on.

"It was so complex that it was a personal challenge for the both of us," Johnson said.

First a financial package was put together. It included thirty-year loans from the federal government and the city of Nashville, a twenty-year industrial revenue bond issue, and private equity. The package totaled $12.5 million. In addition, Gulf Coast received the $1.5 million the GSA turned over for stabilization, making the restoration budget an even $14 million. Gulf Coast became the new owner of the Union Station project. Elkington and Keltner and CRC Equities remained involved but as limited partners whose ownership totaled fifteen percent. Elkington and Keltner would be completely out by opening day.

The city of Nashville legally received the station back from the GSA and leased it to Gulf Coast for ninety years. No agreement

could be reached with the railroad on a price for the shed, so Gulf Coast focused on the station alone.

One of the major problems at the outset was obtaining approvals from watchdog agencies. These agencies on the local, state and federal level were responsible for making sure that preservation standards were met. The transformation of Union Station was a "tax act project," which meant that investors received substantial tax breaks if the work proceeded according to the National Historic Preservation Act. Moore and Johnson had not had to worry much about this kind of thing while building a Shoney's Inn.

The approvals, which proved involved and time consuming, were usually negotiated by Johnson, whose restless energy evoked a sense of the impetuous Major Lewis, and

*Stained glass transoms (below) from the former waiting rooms were removed, repaired and reinstalled in the hotel dining areas. A curved perspective of the stained glass in the vault is shown in the upper right.*

A RUIN TRANSFORMED

Left: *The hotel lobby and the north wall.*

Above: *A modern lighting fixture in the lobby has gilded fretwork behind it. Two angels of commerce in spandrels and sections of the stained glass ceiling are high above.*

101

carried out by Moore, whose style was more subdued. Work on the transformation went forward smoothly under the leadership of Raymond Tomlinson, head superintendent of Moore and Associates, the general contractor.

Ann Reynolds, director of the Metro Historical Commission in Nashville and one of the people responsible for the quality of the preservation work, was impressed by the speed and efficiency with which Moore and Johnson got things done. After all the years of

talk about the station, having people involved with it who actually accomplished something was a breath of fresh air.

The construction work dealt primarily with repairing deterioration and with converting various floors into restaurants, kitchens, a ballroom, administrative and support areas, and one hundred and twenty-eight guest rooms. One of the more challenging tasks was the restoration of the main waiting room. This work began in May, 1986, when the highly

*A workman and the new clocks.*

respected Conrad Schmitt Studios sent Jim
Makovic and his veteran crew to Nashville.
The craftsmen had won a national award the
previous year for decorating the restored
Netherland Plaza in Cincinnati. Their other
projects included the Waldorf-Astoria in New
York and Union Station in St. Louis.

When Makovic and his crew took their
first look at the main waiting room, they saw
a layer of black grit and dirt covering everything. They had a subcontractor erect scaffolding from the tile floor to the wooden ribs of
the stained-glass ceiling. The stained-glass
panels themselves had already been removed
and taken to Emmanuel Studios in Nashville
for cleaning and repair.

Wearing whites and respirators, Makovic
and his men stripped loose paint from the
walls, medallions, cornices, angels, frieze and
other bas-relief work. They blew the surfaces
clean and washed them under strong water
pressure. All plaster surfaces were primed
and then topped off with fresh plaster to
smooth in pits and chips. A second coat of
primer went on and then the finish enameling
began. Makovic compared this smaller Union
Station favorably to the larger one in St. Louis
where he had worked earlier. The art here
was better executed, he said, and a little the-
atrical, which he liked. Talking animatedly
from high on the scaffolding, he swept an
arm towards two nearby angels and said,
"This one is going to have a little more grandeur. It's Nashville. Rhinestones and glitter."

The colors that he and his men would
use in the main waiting room became one of

*Howard Hoover vacuums the leaded glass
on top of the lobby's skylight.*

103

*Gilded fretwork (right), and carved wooden capitals (below, right) decorate the building. When the station was not in use, vandels wrestled several carved crowns (below, middle) off their newel posts. Using one that survived as a model, modern craftsmen made new ones. A geometric pattern (below, left) is found in the tiles on the floor of the portico.*

the significant preservation questions Richard Johnson argued about with Ann Reynolds of the Metro Historical Commission. The original colors had been various shades of green, darker below and becoming lighter as they approached the stained-glass ceiling. Moore and Johnson wanted their hotel to have a brighter look for modern times. Since cinder showers were a thing of the past and the darker colors of the Victorian era no longer needed to hide accumulated smoke and soot, a compromise was worked out. Lighter greens and a pale mauve became the new colors. They belonged to the original color families, but lightened them.

Another painting change involved the ageless angels of Tennessee commerce. The original flesh tones and colored robes had created somewhat cartoonish figures, the con-

*Decorating the north wall are Progress (above, left), who clutches a railroad wheel to his chest, and Time (above, right), who over the years has lost her "thread of life" she spun on opening day.*

*A decorative painter from Conrad Schmitt Studios wets his brush before applying more paint.*

105

temporary reasoning went, and drew greater attention to the angels than they deserved. The point seemed debatable but the contemporary concept held sway; the angels were painted a greyish ocher and gilded. This way they complemented the cornices, brackets and medallions in the upper curves of the vault. Twenty-four-carat gold leafing was applied to much of the raised ornamentation, making the lobby sparkle more than it had in 1900.

While the painters worked on the interior, transformation of the building into a hotel proceeded all around them. The previous spring one hundred and twenty thousand slate roofing shingles had been laid and copper flashing and gutters installed. The streaked and grimy exterior was scrubbed

clean with high-pressure water, revealing the true surface of the Bowling Green limestone once again. During the summer and fall of 1986, crews of carpenters, plumbers, electricians, heating and air conditioning specialists, and others were busy everywhere, from the track level where workmen erected steel for the ceiling of the grand ballroom, to the roof where skylights were installed to protect the stained-glass ceiling when it was put back in. In the northeast room, where fathers had brought their families for Sunday lunches at the turn of the century, craftsmen replicated oak wainscoting. In the former ladies' waiting room, plasterers laid down scratch, brown and finish coats in long sweeping strokes.

Throughout the station, as opening day

*Details on the bas-relief work, such as the bully engine number 108 and the Egyptian pharaoh and his wife, required stripping, washing under pressure, priming, fresh plastering, priming again, enameling, and then gilding to restore them to their original beauty.*

approached, dozens of demanding jobs proceeded simultaneously. Cornice woodworking
was stripped and stained. Tennessee pink
marble, original to the vestibules but removed
for the installation of modern systems, was
trimmed, polished and put back up. Partition
walls came down and new ones were erected.
The entire building, except the main waiting
room, needed a sprinkler system for fire pro-
tection. Modern wiring was installed. Tons of
old piping were torn out and replaced with
new plumbing. To comply with the building
code, the handrail and wrought-iron balustrade at the mezzanine level were raised. Similar safety requirements for the stairways
necessitated the turning of one thousand six
hundred and fifty-two spindles. Longer than
the originals, the spindles dovetailed into new
stair treads and placed the handrail at building code height. Modern craftsmen, impressed by the work of their predecessors
from almost a century earlier, tried to match
its quality and standards.

Friday morning meetings in the office of
Moore and Associates, the general contractor,
brought the superintendents, foremen, sub-
contractors, historic preservation officials,
architects and suppliers together. The previous week's work was critiqued and the following week's work scheduled. The meetings
were often long, loud and lively. Fashioning
each of the hotel's one hundred and twenty-
eight rooms into the exterior, lobby and window constraints demanded exceptional
coordination as every single room was
different.

*A helicopter lifts scaffolding off the tower
of Union Station just before it opens in December, 1986.*

107

Below: *Laid in tile beneath the portico facing Broad Street, this flying wheel symbolized the soaring future of the L & N.*

Right: *Building codes mandated that new spindles be turned for the stairways.*

The hotel opened unofficially in mid-December, 1986, with a black tie dinner in honor of Joe Rodgers, a Nashville businessman and the United States Ambassador to France. Work had not been completed, however, and it continued with a growing sense of urgency. Pressure mounted. Occupancy permits were necessary if investors were to receive their tax credits for the year. A kind of controlled pandemonium gripped Union Station as January 1 approached.

Workmen lugged in furniture, plumbers installed vanities, tiles in the restaurants were cleaned, while in side rooms waiters and waitresses, cooks and other hotel staff were lectured and trained. A marble fountain from Italy went in where the silver cups on chains had been years before. Traditional round

Left: *The Major's Club, one of the hotel's four restaurants, is located in the Station's former fine dining room and named after Major Eugene Lewis and Major John Thomas, president of the NC & St L.*

Above: *Miss Nashville and Miss Louisville reach out for each other as they have done for almost a century.*

clocks appeared in the tower, unsynchronized at first but soon keeping the kind of time that would have pleased Major Lewis. Television, radio and press coverage intensified. Public curiosity mounted as the construction materials in the porte-cochère area disappeared and signs for valet parking invited drivers off Broad Street. Billboards around Nashville carried a large picture of the station and the words "Opening Soon."

The portico on Broad Street, glassed-in, with white linen on the tables and diners in the chairs, confused a few older motorists—had the elegant restaurant of old been resurrected and moved? Those who went inside to eat or just to stare craned their necks to see the replaced stained-glass ceiling. The angels of commerce looked as fresh as the day the girls from Wards' Seminary had dramatized them in real life. Light from overhead was warmly tinted and diffused. People pointed at the clock over Time and Progress, at the bully 108 that artist Doner had sculpted, at the two young ladies above, one a likeness of Major Lewis's daughter Louise.

Occupancy permits were received by January 1, 1987, and everyone working on the station relaxed a little. The dining rooms—in the former ladies' waiting room, the front portico, and the old restaurant location—were busy. Well-known local attorney and writer, Jack Norman, Sr., wrote a nostalgic column

*Four hundred workers and craftsmen worked around the clock, seven days a week, to restore the building and its many architectural details.*

praising "the fact that the old lady of Broad Street had dressed up to serve the modern city in a modern way." He lamented that the sound system did not intone with a heavy voice: "Train Number 6, from New Orleans, Mobile, Birmingham, and all points between, is now loading on track 4. Train Number 10 for Bowling Green, Louisville, Cincinnati and Chicago is now ready for boarding on track 2. Have your tickets ready at gate 1. All aboard, please."

Of the many visitors who came to see the transformed station many were past railroad employees. A few climbed the stairs to the mezzanine and leaned over the balcony, smiling. To them in particular, the station spoke, as Major Lewis had claimed it did on opening day in 1900, with a thousand voices. If they were quiet and thoughtful they could recall some of them: redcaps, ticket clerks, lonely soldiers, girls going off to college. Below, moving on the floor of the main waiting room that was now the hotel lobby, were all kinds of people. Some of these people they knew. Others were strangers. Many of them probably had never even ridden on a train. Union Station would never be the same, but then it had never stayed the same before. It had always been changing, like time itself.

The future and the past intertwined and jutted up like a tower—that was what Union Station had become. It honored those who built it, those who loved and used it, those who fought to save it, and those who transformed it. In a great building the distant past and the foreseeable future had become one.

On December 15, 1986, more than 360 people attended a black tie dinner, the first event in the renovated Union Station, at which Joe Rodgers (right), Nashville businessman and U.S. Ambassador to France, received the first Jack C. Massey (left) Leadership Award.

# Floor Plans

FIRST LEVEL Union Station was a square, one hundred and fifty feet on each side. Surrounding the main waiting room, which was a barrel vault with a sixty-three-foot-high ceiling, were individual waiting rooms, a restaurant and a lunch room. A newsstand, soda fountain, parcel check, barber shop and shoeshine stand provided services to travelers.

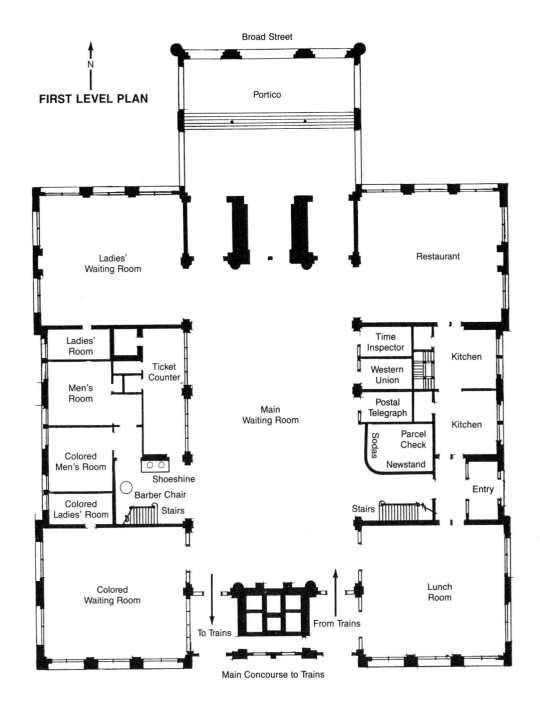

**FIRST LEVEL PLAN**

N

Broad Street

Portico

Ladies' Waiting Room

Restaurant

Ladies' Room

Ticket Counter

Men's Room

Time Inspector

Kitchen

Western Union

Colored Men's Room

Postal Telegraph

Kitchen

Sodas

Parcel Check

Main Waiting Room

Newstand

Shoeshine

Barber Chair

Stairs

Entry

Colored Ladies' Room

Stairs

Colored Waiting Room

To Trains

From Trains

Lunch Room

Main Concourse to Trains

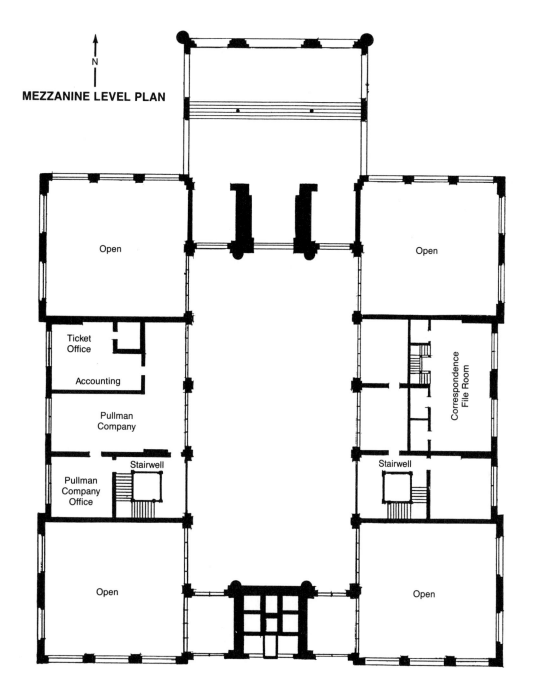

**MEZZANINE LEVEL PLAN**

N

Open

Open

Ticket Office

Accounting

Pullman Company

Correspondence File Room

Pullman Company Office

Stairwell

Stairwell

Open

Open

MEZZANINE LEVEL Between the first and second levels, the offices of the Pullman Company were on the mezzanine. The space was limited because of the high ceilings of the corner rooms on the first level.

SECOND LEVEL The balcony cantilevered out over the main waiting room at this level and proved an excellent place from which to view one's fellow travelers. Railroad personnel occupied the surrounding offices. The stairs of the front tower began here as well. Employees could ascend to Major Lewis's digital clockworks, although travelers were prohibited from the tower.

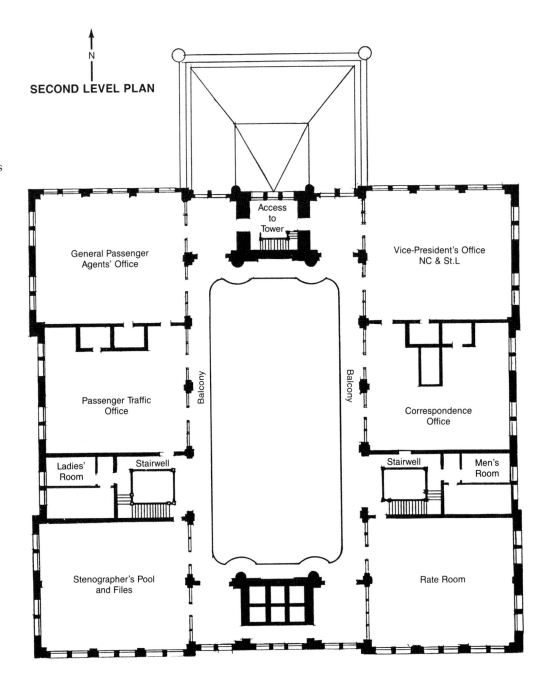

SECOND LEVEL PLAN

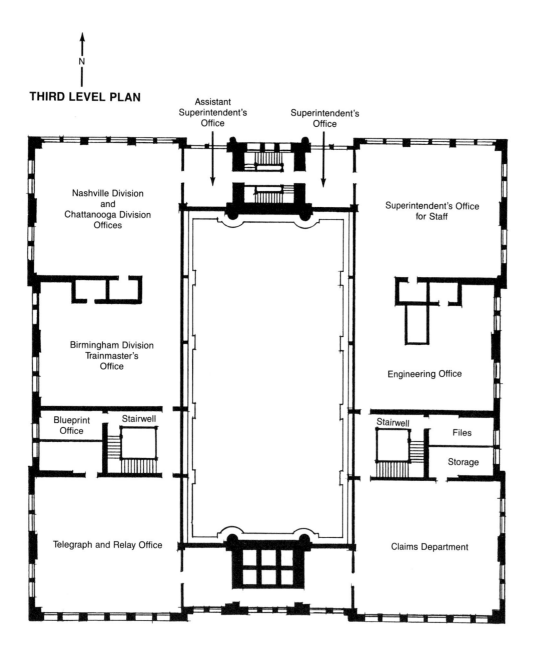

THIRD LEVEL PLAN

Assistant Superintendent's Office

Superintendent's Office

Nashville Division and Chattanooga Division Offices

Superintendent's Office for Staff

Birmingham Division Trainmaster's Office

Engineering Office

Blueprint Office

Stairwell

Stairwell

Files

Storage

Telegraph and Relay Office

Claims Department

THIRD LEVEL The staffs of the superintendent and of several railroad divisions occupied most of the third floor. Private offices for the superintendent and his assistant overlooked Broad Street and the alligator pools. All the offices were heated by ducts that rose from the plenum below the floor of the main waiting room. Ventilation was a matter of opening a window.

# Acknowledgments

Many people contributed stories, insights, memories, photographs and emotions to this book, and to all of them the author is much indebted. This book was much enriched by their collaboration.

In particular he wants to thank Louise Davis, whose timely reporting planted the seed for the eventual saving of Union Station. Nashville architect Michael Emrick and railroad veteran Custis Stamp both shared generously of their time, knowledge and photographs. Mary Glenn Hearne of the Metropolitan Nashville-Davidson County Public Library and her helpful staff frequently steered the author to materials and pictures he otherwise never would have found, as did the staff at the Tennessee State Library and Archives, particularly Wayne Moore.

Raymond Tomlinson, superintendent of construction, guided the author's first tour through the station, and developers Leon Moore and Richard Johnson allowed him free access to meetings, drawings and the site. Public relations director Bernie Sheahan patiently assisted the author through his research. He appreciates their cooperation and thanks them.

Numerous individuals consented to be interviewed. They included Mayor Richard Fulton, H.H. Hendrix, Neill S. Brown, Lewis Frazer, James Patrick, D.W. Wear, Wilbur F. Creighton, Jr., Mary Guill, Fletch Coke, Felix Hoots, Ira L. Bell, Mary Loftin Wilson and Van B. Wilson, Jordan Kinnard, W.A. Anderton, Charlie Warterfield, and Berle Pilsk. Their tales, insights and memories greatly enriched the story.

Color photography courtesy of Union Station Hotel was shot by Juergen Christ, and Nashville native Ed Clark took the riveting World War II photographs. The libraries and several photographers of *The Tennessean* and the *Nashville Banner* also provided excellent photographs.

Larry Stone, who edited the manuscript and ushered the project through from start to finish, has the author's praise for his forthrightness, support and improvements in the text. Mary Anne McNeese, also of Rutledge Hill Press, much eased the search for photographs.

Lastly, the author thanks all those whose voices contributed to *Speaking of Union Station,* an oral history from which he drew liberally.

# Illustrations

Cover illustration copyright © 1983 by George B. Kirchner and used by permission.
Page 3 Photograph, *ca.* 1901, courtesy of Michael Emrick

**Chapter 1 An Opening Conflict**
Page 10 Photograph, *ca.* 1895, courtesy of Lewis Frazer
Page 11 Photograph, 1900, University of Louisville Photographic Archives, courtesy of Michael Emrick
Page 12 Photograph, *ca.* 1875, Tennessee State Library and Archives
Page 13 Photograph, *ca.* 1897, courtesy of Lewis Frazer
Page 14 Photograph, 1897, Tennessee State Library and Archives
Page 15 Photograph, 1897, Tennessee State Library and Archives

**Chapter 2 Architectural Design**
Page 18 Photograph, Carnegie Library of Pittsburgh
Page 19 Blueprint, 1896, Office of Chief Engineer of L&N Railroad, courtesy of Michael Emrick
Page 20 Photograph, 1900, Nashville Room, Metropolitan Nashville-Davidson County Public Library

**Chapter 3 Building A Landmark**
Page 22 (top) Photograph, 1898, University of Louisville Photographic Archives, courtesy of Michael Emrick
(bottom) Photograph, 1899, University of Louisville Photographic Archives, courtesy of Michael Emrick
Page 23 (top) Photograph, 1899, University of Louisville Photographic Archives, courtesy of Michael Emrick
(bottom) Photograph, 1899, University of Louisville Photographic Archives, courtesy of Michael Emrick
Page 24 Photograph, 1899, University of Louisville Photographic Archives, courtesy of Michael Emrick
Page 25 Photograph, *ca.* 1919, Tennessee State Library and Archives
Page 26 Mr. Hill photograph, *ca.* 1903, Joe Horton Studios

Page 27 *Nashville Banner* photograph, 1986, by Mark Lyons
Page 28 Jack E. Boucher photograph, 1973, Historical American Building Survey
Page 29 Blueprint, 1896, Office of Chief Engineer of L&N Railroad, courtesy of Rick Stoll
Page 30 (left) Joe Sherman photograph, 1986
(right) Photograph, *ca.* 1898, courtesy of Lewis Frazer
Page 31 Photograph, *ca.* 1901, courtesy of Michael Emrick
Page 32 Photograph, *ca.* 1978, courtesy of Michael Emrick

**Chapter 4 Alligator Pools, A Digital Clock, and Mercury**
Page 34 Photograph courtesy of The Bettman Archive
Page 35 Drawing by L. L. Gamble, courtesy of George B. Kirchner
Page 36 Photograph, 1950, by Don Cravens, courtesy of *The Tennessean*
Page 37 Watercolor by Major E. C. Lewis, *ca.* 1895, courtesy of Lewis Frazer
Page 38 Photograph, *ca.* 1950, *Tennessean* library
Page 39 Custis Stamp photograph, 1952

**Chapter 5 The City and Its Station**
Page 42 Photograph *ca.* 1905, Nashville Room, Metropolitan Nashville-Davidson County Public Library
Page 43 Photograph *ca.* 1905, Nashville Room, Metropolitan Nashville-Davidson County Public Library
Page 44 Chamber of Commerce poster, *ca.* 1900, Tennessee State Library and Archives
Page 45 Photograph, *ca.* 1910, Tennessee State Library and Archives
Page 46 Photograph, *ca.* 1903, Tennessee State Library and Archives
Page 47 Photograph, *ca.* 1903, Nashville Room, Metropolitan Nashville-Davidson County Public Library
Page 48 Calvert Brothers photograph, *ca.* 1900, Tennessee State Library and Archives

**Chapter 6  The Only Way to Travel**
Page  50  Photograph *ca.* 1924, courtesy of Custis Stamp
Page  51  L&N timetable, 1907, courtesy of H. H. Hendrix
Page  52  L&N timetable, 1907, courtesy of H. H. Hendrix
Page  53  Photograph, *ca.* 1940, courtesy of Mary Loftin Wilson
Page  55  NC&St L timetable, 1949, courtesy of Ira Bell
Page  56  NC&St L timetable, 1949, courtesy of Ira Bell
Page  57  Photograph, 1919, Tennessee State Library and Archives

**Chapter 7  Working There**
Page  60  Photograph, *ca.* 1925, courtesy of *L&N Magazine* publisher
Page  61  Photograph, *ca.* 1940, courtesy of Mary Loftin Wilson
Page  63  John E. Hood photograph, 1942, courtesy of Mary Loftin Wilson
Page  64  *The Official Guide of the Railways,* 1962, courtesy of Mary Loftin Wilson
Page  65  Blueprint, 1896, courtesy of Metropolitan Historical Commission
Page  66  Jack E. Boucher photograph, 1973, Historical American Buildings Survey
Page  69  Jack E. Boucher photograph, 1973, Historical American Buildings Survey

**Chapter 8  Hard Times, Great Visitors**
Page  72  Photograph, *ca.* 1933, courtesy of Rick Stoll
Page  73  Photograph, 1934, *Tennessean* library
Page  74  Photograph, 1938, Vanderbilt University *Commodore*
Page  75  Photograph, 1934, Nashville Room, Metropolitan Nashville-Davidson County Public Library
Page  76  Photograph, 1938, *Tennessean* library

**Chapter 9  World War II**
Page  78  Ed Clark photograph, 1942, Tennessee State Library and Archives
Page  79  Ed Clark photograph, 1942, Tennessee State Library and Archives
Page  80  Photograph, 1943, courtesy of Mary Loftin Wilson
Page  81  Ed Clark photograph, 1942, Tennessee State Library and Archives
Page  82  Ed Clark photograph, 1942, Tennessee State Library and Archives
Page  83  Ed Clark photograph, 1942, Tennessee State Library and Archives
Page  84  Ed Clark photograph, 1942, Tennessee State Library and Archives

**Chapter 10  From Pullmans to Pontiacs**
Page  86  Photograph, *ca.* 1950, *Tennessean* library
Page  87  (left) Custis Stamp photograph, 1950
        (right) Custis Stamp photograph, 1949
Page  88  Custis Stamp photograph, 1953
Page  89  Custis Stamp photograph, 1950
Page  90  NC&St L timetable, *ca.* 1955, courtesy of Ira Bell

**Chapter 11  Pigeons and Politicians**
Page  92  *Nashville Banner* photograph, 1979, by Bob Ray
Page  93  *Nashville Banner* photograph, 1986, by Anthony Lathrop
Page  94  Photograph, 1978, courtesy of Senator Jim Sasser and *Tennessean* Library
Page  95  Dan Loftin photograph, 1983, *Tennessean* library
Page  96  *Nashville Banner* photograph, 1980, by Don Foster
Page  97  *Nashville Banner* photograph, 1979, by Don Foster
Page  98  *Nashville Banner* photograph, 1983, by Bill Goodman

**Chapter 12  A Ruin Transformed**
Page 100  (top left) Joe Sherman photograph, 1986
        (bottom left and right) Photographs by Juergen Christ, 1986, courtesy of Union Station Hotel
Page 101  (left and right) Photographs by Juergen Christ, courtesy of Union Station Hotel
Page 102  Photograph by Kathleen Smith-Barry, 1986
Page 103  Photograph by Kathleen Smith-Barry, 1986
Page 104  (bottom left) Joe Sherman photograph, 1986
        (all others) Photographs by Juergen Christ, 1986, courtesy of Union Station Hotel
Page 105  (top) Photographs by Juergen Christ, 1986, courtesy of Union Station Hotel
        (bottom) Joe Sherman photograph, 1986
Page 106  (left) Joe Sherman photograph, 1986
        (right) Photograph by Kathleen Smith-Barry, 1986
Page 107  *Nashville Banner* photograph, 1986, by Jonathan Newton
Page 108  Photographs by Juergen Christ, 1986, courtesy of Union Station Hotel
Page 109  Photographs by Juergen Christ, 1986, courtesy of Union Station Hotel
Page 110  (left) Photograph by Kathleen Smith-Barry, 1986
        (right) Joe Sherman photograph, 1986
Page 111  *Nashville Banner* photograph, 1986, by Larry McCormack
Page 112  Photographs by Juergen Christ, courtesy of Union Station Hotel

# References

Anonymous, *Major Eugene Castner Lewis, A Tribute,* (Nashville: privately published, 1934)

Edwin W. Alexander, *Down at the Depot, American Railroad Stations from 1831-1920* (New York: Clarkson N. Potter, 1970)

Thomas B. Brumbaugh, "The Architecture of Nashville's Union Station," in *Tennessee Historical Quarterly,* vol. XXVII, Spring-Summer, 1968

_____, Martha I. Strayhorn, and Gary G. Gore (eds.), *Architecture of Middle Tennessee* (Nashville: Vanderbilt University Press, 1974)

David Cohen (ed.) *Long Steel Rail, The Railroad in American Folksong* (Urbana: University of Illinois Press, 1981)

Deborah Cooney (ed.), *Speaking of Union Station* (Nashville: Union Station Trust Fund, 1977)

Louise Davis, "All Aboard for Union Station," in *The Tennesseean Magazine,* February 9, 1975

_____, "Alligators and Clocks," in *The Tennessean Magazine,* March 3, 1975

Don H. Doyle, *Nashville in the New South, 1880-1930* (Knoxville: The University of Tennessee Press, 1985)

_____, *Nashville Since the 1920s* (Knoxville: The University of Tennessee Press, 1985)

John Egerton, *Nashville: The Faces of Two Centuries* (Nashville: PlusMedia Incorporated, 1979)

Michael Emrick, Doug Yorke, and Joseph Herndon, "Historical Structure Report, Union Station, Nashville, Tennessee," an architectural conservator's report (Nashville: Building Conservation Technology, 1980)

Eleanor Graham (ed.), *Nashville, A Short History and Selected Buildings* (Nashville: Historical Commission of Metropolitan Nashville-Davidson County, 1974)

Mary Guill, "Color Documentation for Main Floor Areas of Union Station, Nashville, Tennessee," an historical report (Nashville: Guill, Inc., 1986)

Phillip M. Hamer (ed.), *Tennessee, A History, Vol. IV* (New York: The American Historical Society, Inc., 1933)

Kincaid A. Herr, *The Louisville and Nashville Railroad* (Louisville: L&N Magazine Publisher, 1943)

James A. Hoobler (dir.) *Art Work of Nashville* (Nashville: Tennessee Historical Society reprint, 1981)

William H. Jordy, *American Buildings and Their Architects* (Garden City: Doubleday & Company, Inc., 1972)

Lou Nash, "Top Man Over Nashville's Union Station," in *The L&N Employes' Magazine*, August, 1946

Jeffrey Karl Ochsner, *H. H. Richardson, Complete Architectural Works* (Cambridge, Massachusetts: The MIT Press, 1984)

David Paine, *Downtown Nashville Art and Architecture, Three Walking Tours* (Nashville: Metropolitan Historical Commission)

James Gregory Rubin, Nancy Stout, and others, *Temple of Justice* (New York: Architectural League of New York, 1977)

Custis L. Stamp, "Top Man for 50 Years," in *The Tennessean Magazine*, June 14, 1950

William Waller (ed.), *Nashville in the 1890s* (Nashville: Vanderbilt University Press, 1970)

————, *Nashville, 1900 to 1910* (Nashville: Vanderbilt University Press, 1972)

Joseph Watterson, *Architecture, A Short History* (New York: W.W. Norton & Co., 1968)

# Index

Alex, Nell, (photo, 80)
Allegheny County Courthouse (Pittsburgh, PA), 17, 18, (photo, 19)
Alligators, 19, 25, 33–34, 41, 68, 91
Alimini Co., 28
Amtrak, 90, 91
Anderton, W. A., 63–64, 66, 67, 82
Anderton, W. A., father-in-law of, 63
Arcade, 43, (photo, 47)
*Architecture of Middle Tennessee*, 91
*Azalea*, 54

Bass, Dorothy Davis, (photo, 80)
Baxter, Jere, 9, 10, 12, 15, 26, 45, 54
Bellevue (community), 53
Belmont, August, 3, 12, 13, 19
Bernhardt, Sarah, 48
Berry Field, 85
"Black Bottom," 44
Boner, Bill, 99
Bowling Green, KY, 21
Braid, J. W., 35
Brame, Vivian Whitehead, (photo, 80)
Brumbach, Thomas B., 91
Bryan, William Jennings, 48
Burton, Andrew Mizell, 44
Byrns, Joseph W., 71

*Cannonball Express*, 56
Capone, Al, 75–76
Carter, Jimmy, 94
Caruso, Enrico, 48
Cauvin, Saidee, 12–13
Centennial Exposition of 1897, 12, 15, 16, 23, 33, 37, 43, 44
Centennial Park, 16, 66
Chattanooga, TN, 49
Chaplain, Charlie, 48
*Chat*, 47
Cheek, Joel Owlsley, 44
Cheek-Neal Coffee Co., 45
Christ Episcopal Church, 41
Clock, digital, 32, 33, 34–37, 68, 91
Coats, Carrie J. Fitzgerald, (photo, 80)
Coke, Alice, (photo, 94)
Coke, Fletch, 93, 94, (photo, 94)
CRC Equities, 98, 99
Cumberland Iron Works, 54
Cumberland River, 41
Cummins Station, 45
Cunningham, Carl, 69
Customs House, 41, 93

Davant, Alice, (photo, 80)
Davis, Dorothy. *See* Bass, Dorothy Davis
Davis, Era Strane, (photo, 80)
Davis, Etta, (photo, 80)
Davis, "Hogshead," 61
Davis, Louise, 91, 93, 99
Dean, "Dizzy," 85
Depot Bill, 16, 26
Dickson, TN, 49
*Dixie Flyer*, 52, 54, 65, 75, (photo, 50)
Doner, J. M., 28, 30, 110
Dudley Field, 74

Elkington and Keltner Development, 98, 99
Emmanuel Studios, 103
Emrick, Michael, 94

Finley, Mrs. Thanial, (photo, 80)
First National Bank, 43
Fisk University, 71
Fitzgerald, Carrie J. *See* Coats, Carrie J. Fitzgerald
Fleming, "Tootsie," 61
*Floridian*, 96
Fulton, Richard, 73, 97, 98, (photo, 98)

Geddes, James, 33
General Services Administration, 93, 94, 95, 96, 97, 98
*Georgian*, 54

Gould, Jay, 59
Grand Ole Opry, 41, 48, 93
Grubbs, Nancy Waddell, (photo, 80)
Gulf Coast Development, Inc., 99, 100

Harbison, Christine, (photo, 80)
Harding, Warren G., 68
Head, James, H., 10, 12, 13, 45, 91
Heflin, Roberta Shumate, (photo, 80)
"Hell's Half Acre," 44
Hermitage Hotel, 93
Hicks, Betty, (photo, 80)
Hill, H. G., 44
Historic Nashville, 93, 97, 98
Hodges, James Baxter, 37, 38
Hoover, Howard, (photo, 103)
Howse, Hilary, (photo, 75)
Hume-Fogg High School, 41
*Hummingbird*, 54, 85
Hutton, Fred, 93

John Henry, 59, 61
Johnson, Richard, 99, 100, 102, 105
Jones, "Casey," 56, 59
Jones, Sam P., 41
Jordan, W. E., 23-24, 38
Joslin, Jane. *See* Terry, Jane Joslin
Junior League of Nashville, 93

Keaton, Flossie, (photo, 80)
King, Mary Gilbert. *See* Mathis, Mary Gilbert
    King
Kinnard, J. J., 83

*L&N Magazine*, 23
LaFarge, John, 28
Lake Watauga, 16
Lebanon, TN, 49, 86, 88

Lewis, Anita, (photo, 30)
Lewis, Eugene Castner, 9, 10, 12, 14, 15, 16, 19,
    20, 21, 23, 24, 25, 26, 28, 32, 33, 34, 35, 36,
    37, 38, 39, 40, 44, 45, 48, 54-55, 58, 68, 85,
    98, 100, 109, 110, (photo, 10); home of,
    (photo, 13)
Lewis, Floy, (photo, 30)
Lewis, Louise, 28, 110, (photo, 30)
Lewis, Margaretta, (photo, 30)
Lewis, Pauline, 14
Life & Casualty Insurance Corp., 44
Lightfoot, W. A., (photo, 80)
Lindsey, Martha, 53-54
Little Market Basket (grocery store), 81
Loftin, H. W., (photos, 61, 80)
Loftin, Mary Harding, *See* Wilson, Mary Harding
    Loftin
Long, Huey P., 74, (photo, 75)
Louisville, KY, 10, 49, 73
Luminous Prism Co., 28, 30

Makovic, Jim, 103
Massey, Jack C., Leadership Award, 111
Mathis, Mary Gilbert King, (photo, 80)
Maxwell House hotel, 13, 46, 71
McAlister, Hill, 71, (photo, 73)
McCanless, James, 57
McGowan, Lorraine, (photo, 80)
McKinley, William, 16
McLister, Frances, 12-13
"Men's Quarter," 45-46, (photo, 46)
Mercury, 10, 13, 19, 23, 24, 26, 33, 36, 37-40, 41,
    68, 70, 86, 91, (photos, 36, 37, 38, 39)
Metro Historical Commission, 102, 105
Mohawk & Hudson Railroad, 55-56
Montfort, Richard, 19-20
Moore, Leon, 99, 102, 105
Moore and Associates, 102, 107

Moran, Ellen, *See* Pinson, Ellen Moran
Mount Olivet Cemetery, 58
Moynihan, Patrick, 94
Murfreesboro, TN, 49

Napier, James C., 44
*Nashville Banner*, 2, 40
*Nashville Daily Sun*, 15
Nation, Carrie, 48
Nelms, V. T., 82
Nelson & Brothers, 28
"New Shops," 62
*1900 Limited*, 28, 30
Noel, Jeannette Acklen, 81-82
Norman, Jack, Sr., 110

Ogilvie, Mabel, (photo, 80)
Old Hickory Powder Plant, 57-58
One Cent Savings Bank, 44
Opryland USA, 93

Parthenon, 15, 16, 38, (photo, 15)
Petty, Thelma, 59
Pfeiffer, Norman, 93
Pinkleton, W. W., 75-76
Pinson, Ellen Moran, (photo, 80)
Polk, J. P., 68, 81
Proxmire, William, 98
Public Square, 43

Radnor Lake, 62-63
"Railroad Bill," 54, 59, 61
*Railroad Guide*, 78
Ray, Ruby, (photo, 80)
Red Cross Canteen, 80-82
Reeves, Watina. *See* Schoenberger, Watina Reeves
*Reusing Railroad Stations*, 93

Reynolds, Ann, 102, 105
Richardson, Henry Hobson, 17–18, 20, 24, 28
Rodgers, Joe, 108, (photo, 111)
Rooney, Elynor, (photo, 80)
Roosevelt, Eleanor, 71, (photos, 73, 76)
Roosevelt, Franklin D., 71, 74, 83–84, (photo, 73)
Ryman, Tom, 41
Ryman Auditorium, 41, 85, 93, (photo, 48). *See also* Union Tabernacle

St. Louis, 73
Sanders, Mamie, (photo, 80)
Sasser, James, 94, 95, 96
Schlosser, Marianna, (photo, 80)
Schlosser, Roberta, (photo, 80)
Schmitt, Conrad, Studios, 103, 105
Schoenberger, Watina Reeves, (photo, 80)
Schweitzer, Jane. *See* Smith, Jane Schweitzer
Sheraton-Nashville Hotel, 95, 97
Shumate, Roberta. *See* Heflin, Roberta Shumate
Slator, Morris. *See* "Railroad Bill"
Smith, Al, 68
Smith, Jane Schweitzer, (photo, 80)

Smith, Milton, 10, 13, 28, 36
Smith, Milton, daughter of, 28
Solomon, Jay, 94, 95, 96
Southern Turf, 46
*Southwind*, 54
*Speaking of Union Station*, 93
Stahlman, James G., 33, 40
Stahlman, Mary, 33, 51
Stamp, Custis, 40
Stevenson, Vernon K., 14
Sycamore, TN, 14

Tennessee Central Railroad, 10, 12, 15, 45, 54, 91
Tennessee State Capitol, 41, 44, 71
*The Tennessean*, 74, 96
*The Tennessean Magazine*, 91
Terminal Company, 26
Terry, Jane Joslin, (photo, 80)
Thomas, John W., 3, 109
Thompson, John, 74
Tomlinson, Raymond, 102
Trinity Church (Boston, MA), 17, 28
Tullahoma, TN, 49

Union Tabernacle, 41. *See also* Ryman Auditorium
United Service Organization (USO), 80–82
U. S. Senate Committee on Public Works, (photo, 94)
USO. *See* United Service Organization
Utopia Hotel, 46

Vanderbilt, William Henry, 59
Vanderbilt Commodores, 74–75
Vassar, Jane, (photo, 80)
Vaughan, MS, 56
Vauxhall Flats, 41

WSM (radio station), 48
Waddell, Nancy. *See* Grubbs, Nancy Waddell
Ward's Seminary for Young Ladies, 9, 12, 93, 110
Warren, Sarah, (photo, 80)
Watts, "Friday," 61
West, Mae, 85
West Side Park, 16
Whitaker, Alma, (photo, 80)
Whitehead, Vivian, *See* Brame, Vivian Whitehead
Wilson, Mary Harding Loftin, 78–79, (photo, 80)
Wilson, Van B., 66–67, 78